# Excellence in Teaching and Learning

## Bridging the Gaps in Theory, Practice, and Policy

Edited by
Adnan Salhi

Published in cooperation with the Association of Teacher Educ

ROWMAN & LITTLEFIELD EDUCATION, I
Lanham • New York • Toronto • Plymouth, UK

Published in the United States of America
by Rowman & Littlefield Education
A Division of Rowman & Littlefield Publishers, Inc.
A wholly owned subsidiary of The Rowman & Littlefield Publishing Group, Inc.
4501 Forbes Boulevard, Suite 200, Lanham, Maryland 20706
www.rowmaneducation.com

Estover Road
Plymouth PL6 7PY
United Kingdom

Published in cooperation with the Association of Teacher Educators.

British Library Cataloguing in Publication Information Available

**Library of Congress Cataloging-in-Publication Data**

Excellence in teaching and learning : bridging the gaps in theory, practice, and policy /
edited by Adnan Salhi.
    p.   cm.
Includes bibliographical references.
ISBN-13: 978-1-57886-510-9 (cloth : alk. paper)
ISBN-10: 1-57886-510-7 (cloth : alk. paper)
ISBN-13: 978-1-57886-519-2 (pbk. : alk. paper)
ISBN-10: 1-57886-519-0 (pbk. : alk. paper)
    1. Teachers—Training of. 2. Effective teaching. 3. Multicultural education.   I. Salhi,
Adnan, 1949–

LB1707.E93 2006
371.102—dc22                                                     2006014665

# Contents

## Part III. Diversity, Teaching, and Learning

# Preface

$\mathcal{T}$his book is not only about schools and teachers in our neighborhoods, even though it began there. It started amid the exciting times when I attended professional conferences, listened to speeches, and was affected by policies that influenced teaching and learning at many different levels. Because I have been active for years in educational agencies, it was natural for me and the other colleagues I work with to pitch in. A golden opportunity emerged when I chaired the Conference on Excellence in Teaching and Learning and I noticed the many exciting and valuable ideas the participants submitted. All those who presented in the conference were invited to submit finished papers based on what they submitted. These submissions were blind reviewed for the purpose of publishing them in a book that will serve the purpose of bridging the theory, practice, and policy gap that our educational agencies have been suffering from for long.

The inaugural issue was simple. All I did was to draw together classroom strategies, research, and suggested policies about achieving "excellence in teaching and learning." Why did I adopt the theme "Excellence in Teaching and Learning" first for the conference and then for this book? The term may have been used in other places for similar or different reasons. In the case of this book, the term is used to mean a path that leads our children, our teachers, and our schools to do what they are really capable of doing in order to continue their endeavor of doing their best to improve the quality of human lives. That is why I have borrowed and capitalized the term "Excellence in Teaching and Learning" as an emblem of serious, thoughtful, informed, and responsible alliance between all those concerned and involved with the process of teaching and learning.

In assembling contributions from cross-curriculum veteran and experienced educators, a clear agreement appeared on what excellence means and how to bridge the theory, practice, and policy gap. The chapter authors in this book have stellar reputations for using what methodology they write about. They are well accomplished as teachers and teacher educators. Even though the chapters in this book do not have to be read sequentially, they are arranged to make it easy for the readers to see the connections between them. The book starts with an insightful discussion of the ideological underpinnings of discourses on bridging the theory, practice, and policy gap for achieving excellence in teaching and learning. The following chapters provide a wide spectrum of strategies for achieving excellence in teaching and learning and bridging the theory, practice, and policy gap in education. The first part of the book offers practical approaches and research-based hands-on applications that deal with literacy across the curriculum, technology, and diversity.

The second part of the book provides research-based approaches for improving teacher quality and teacher preparation in the short and long terms. Models of these research methods have been provided for practical applications.

The last part of this volume focuses on the ever increasingly important issue in our society in general and our schools in particular—diversity. In this part, we included one chapter that provides a practical strategy for dealing with diversity, another chapter that provides a theoretical framework for understanding diversity, and a chapter that documents where our schools and society stand on diversity issues and where we might be heading on this issue after September 11.

I see this volume as a way of beginning a series of books that will be put in the hands of all those concerned with and care about teaching and learning. It is my hope that teachers, teacher educators, parents, staff developers, administrators, future teachers, and politicians will find this book valuable on the journey to achieving excellence.

—Adnan Salhi

# I

# TEACHING AND LEARNING STRATEGIES

# Bridging the Theory, Practice, and Policy Gap for Achieving Excellence in Teaching and Learning

*P. Rudy Mattai and Jacqueline M. Williams*

*The discourse on bridging the theory, practice, and policy gap for achieving excellence in teaching and learning has been a perennial problem in the academy for almost the entire period of formal activities regarding teaching and learning. However, there has been greater focus on such issues within the world as population shifts and radical demographic changes call into question the issues of equity and equality. Additionally, there have been great efforts largely by politicians to invoke measures of accountability; invariably such efforts are surrogates for bridging the theory, practice, and policy gap. This chapter looks at some of the ideological underpinnings of discourses on bridging this gap and alludes to some of the obstacles that must be addressed.*

## INTRODUCTION

The notion of bridging the theory, practice, and policy gap for achieving excellence in teaching and learning appears at first blush an oxymoron if not virtually an impracticality, especially to those of us who have labored in its trenches for what seems an eternity. It is not without contention among theorists, practitioners, and policy makers in the arena of teaching and learning that the primary spatial environments in which such activities manifest themselves, viz., schooling, are by their very nature bastions of conservatism. A partial though substantive explanation for such phenomena may be attributed to the sociocultural, political, and economic antecedents that gave rise to schooling and more particularly to schooling that is influenced by Western philosophical and ideological models.

What is interesting is that such analyses are not latent; indeed, such analyses have been referred to perennially and have withstood the ebbs and flows of time. Foster (1968) points out rather poignantly almost a half a century ago that

> In most societies educational institutions whether formal or informal, have a dual function; they are both homogenizing and differentiating agencies. In the broadest sense they are concerned with the inculcation of values and appropriate modes of behaviour and the teaching of skills which prepare the individual to participate effectively as an adult member of a community. . . . However, such an approach ignores the fact that educational institutions are also differentiating agencies. . . . Where formal educational institutions begin to appear, it is likely that they operate no less as differentiating institutions. (p. 6)

This "differentiating function" of which Foster (1968) speaks has largely gone unchallenged as one of the pivotal factors that may explain the failure of theory, practice, and policy in achieving excellence in teaching and learning. Carnoy (1974) extrapolated Foster's (1968) position almost a quarter century ago in his classic piece, *Education as Cultural Imperialism*. According to Carnoy (1974), there is a presumption among the large majority of the populaces in both developed and developing countries that there is a definite relationship between the level of education and liberation and, by implication, a "civilizing" agent. Carnoy, drawing the parallel social and cultural reproduction process *par excellence* between schooling in developed and developing countries alike, argues:

> far from acting as a liberator, Western formal education came to most countries as part of imperialist domination. It was consistent with the goals of imperialism: the economic and political control of the people in one country by the dominant class in another . . . the educational system was no more just or equal than the economy and society itself . . . because schooling was organized to develop and maintain . . . an inherently inequitable and unjust organization of production and political power. (p. 3)

Indeed, analyzing the very manner in which schooling is funded in most societies, particularly in the United States of America, it is really no neurological feat to conclude that residential location and family circumstances—often translated as life chances—are fairly dependable variables in predicting the extent to which there will or will not be efficacious outcomes in theory, practice, and policy so far as excellence in teaching and learning are concerned.

But the preceding discourse should not be misconstrued as the analysis of "radical leftists" or that it has been overcome by legislation on behalf of those who have been marginalized in developed and developing countries alike. A plethora of literature over the last several years has enunciated the same genre of analysis including but not limited to the writings of Bowles, Gintis, and

Groves (2005); Carnoy, Jacobsen, and Mishel (2005); Delpit and Kilgour Dowdy (2003); Fischman, McLaren, Sünker, and Lankshear (2004); Gay (2000); Gordon (2000); Ladson-Billings (1994); Spring (2005); Orfield and Kurlaender (2001); Nieto (1999); and more. While this genre of literature has emphasized the disparity between those who are marginalized and the failures of theory, practice, and policy in teaching and learning to bridge that seeming chasm, they have failed to emphasize the inherent "differentiating function" of the educational institutions charged with providing, even in a benign manner, a perceived homogenizing aspect of education.

In fact, reading the genre of literature almost persuades one to believe that by merely reforming the curricula and/or pedagogy of formal schooling such institutions may indeed bridge the theory, practice, and policy gap to achieve excellence in teaching and learning. This piece negates such a position and argues instead that unless the very structures and their supporting political ideologies are revamped, there will be a perpetual failure in bridging that gap. The recent enactment of the No Child Left Behind (NCLB) Act (2001) and the standards reform discourses are usurped in taking such a position, so this chapter shows how bridging the theory, practice, and policy gap is not addressed in such actions, thereby guaranteeing a disconnect between theory, practice, and policy and achieving excellence in teaching and learning.

## BUILT-IN FAILURES IN BRIDGING THE GAP OR BUSINESS AS USUAL?

One of the watersheds in the history of the amalgamation of theory, practice, and policy in achieving excellence in teaching and learning is ostensibly the emergence of NCLB and the presumptions by those who have engineered it. It is worth noting that the very machinations undergirding both the development of NCLB and its *modus operandi* post-legislation are not often taken into consideration by those who espouse bridging the theory, practice, and policy gap. In fact, a blind eye is being turned toward one of the most intractable variables in the failure to bridge the gap, that is, the political sphere of activities.

Simpson, LaCava, and Graner (2004), in a rather interesting piece, "The No Child Left Behind Act: Challenges and Implications for Educators," summarize the potency of political maneuverings and the virtual absence of professional educators and scholars in both development and implementation of NCLB:

> The No Child Left behind (NCLB) Act of 2001, signed into law by President George W. Bush on January 8, 2002, is the most noteworthy of recent

congressional attempts to improve student achievement and otherwise reform elementary and secondary education programs in the United States.
. . . The central overarching theme of NCLB is accountability, including accountability for positive academic outcomes and related results. To be sure,
the idea of *accountability* is replete in NCLB, and it is this concept that forms
the foundation of the act. NCLB holds individual schools, districts, and
states accountable for improvements in student achievement, with particular emphasis on closing the achievement gap between high-and low-
performing students and children and youths from disadvantaged groups
and minority populations . . . including those with special needs . . . by the
conclusion of the 2013–2014 school year. . . . Individual states developing
plans to ensure that all teachers of core academic subjects are "highly qualified" by the end of the 2005–2006 academic year. . . . [And, ostensibly pro-
moting] the use of effective educational practice based on *scientifically based
research* (SBR), which is defined as methods that have met rigorous standards
and that have been shown, when correctly applied, to reliably yield positive
results . . . [and] that parents are afforded expanded opportunities for decision making and other amplified alternatives associated with their children's
education. (pp. 68, 69)

The very manner in which NCLB came into being raises some pertinent
questions regarding theory, practice, and policy. Reference has already been
made to the political undertones of NCLB. However, the political machinations were not devoid of judicial implications that raise serious questions for
bridging the theory, practice, and policy gap. DeBray (2005), in a review of a
judicial battle between the Pinellas County, Florida, school system and the federal court's oversight of desegregation and the implementation of NCLB's
public school choice provisions, pellucidly manifests some of the obstacles to
achieving excellence in teaching and learning. Referring to the issues as conflicts between the federal mandates as determined by Congress and the rulings
of the federal courts, DeBray (2005) enumerates three major conflictual issues:

- The legal conflict between two federal mandates, desegregation and
  school choice;
- the political tension arising between local and federal officials resulting
  from the changing nature of federal authority with respect to desegregation; and
- the policy-related conflict between test-based accountability and desegregation in southern school systems. (pp. 170–71)

The disconnect is not merely a lack of agreement among the various parties concerned with the presumed aspirations of the framers and parties of interests in creating the NCLB. It is much more incisive and according to De-
Bray (2005):

> From a legal standpoint, this case involves a conflict between a federal court
> and a federal statute whose resolution is found in the supremacy clause of
> the constitution. The regulations for NCLB specify that local educational
> agencies must offer a choice of public schools to parents of all students in
> schools failing to make adequate yearly progress (AYP) as defined by the
> state for 2 or more consecutive years. The law requires districts to give par-
> ents a choice of more than one school, and to give priority to the lowest
> achieving children from low-income families. According to the regulations,
> districts may not use insufficient capacity as a reason to not offer choice;
> they state that districts must create additional capacity or provide choices of
> other schools. (p. 171)

At a superficial level, it appears as though there is recourse for parents of
children who are most likely to be affected by inferior schooling, especially if
one takes at face value the notion that districts will give parents a choice of
schools and give low achieving children first priority. However, there is a presumption that such parents have cultural capital that permits them to cognitively
address the underlying factors that contribute to their children's low-achieving
status in school and the material resources to confront the hegemonic practices
of the state apparatuses primarily through the judicial system. Greenberger
(2005) poses for us the real barriers to such expectations in what is rather an
ironical position in the supremacy clause of the constitution:

> Federalism as a principle of political organization is meant to protect and
> promote individual liberty by protecting the autonomy of state government
> against the accumulation of centralized power and thereby providing in-
> creased control over one's personal environment. However, as Wechsler ar-
> gued, and the Supreme Court ruled in *Garcia v. San Antonio Metropolitan
> Transit Authority*, state participation and influence in the federal legislative
> process "ensures that laws that unduly burden the States will not be prom-
> ulgated," and that "State sovereign interests . . . are more properly protected
> by procedural safeguards inherent in the structure of the federal system than
> by judicially created limitations on federal power." (p. 1045)

Indeed, Greenberger (2005) posits the ironic, if not impossible and highly
improbable, situation more clearly when she notes that

> For defenders of federalism, the value of state and local government does
> not lie solely in the institutions themselves, but in their ability to safeguard
> liberty and produce desirable results such as innovation, participation, and
> responsiveness. Where governments fail to produce these benefits through
> traditional political methods, other means are necessary. . . . And when eval-
> uating congressional intent, it should be remembered that federal statutes
> often address national needs created by an imbalance of political power that

makes private enforcement necessary. [However,] statutes must be interpreted in light of larger principles, [since] the Supreme Court has explicitly stated that *the appropriate balance of power between federal and state governments in shaping public policy is one principle that is left to political, not judicial, judgment.* (pp. 1051–52, emphasis added)

This collision between federal mandates and the political will at the state level is amply demonstrated in two case studies. Reference has already been made to DeBray's (2005) review of a judicial battle between the Pinellas County school system and the federal court. The second case study is discussed by Wright (2005) with respect to English Language Learners (ELL) in the state of Arizona. Wright (2005) concludes that

New issues emerge as the requirements of each policy become intertwined and as each is interpreted and implemented by various policy actors at the state level. Within this intersection, many of the accommodations become nullified, that is, an accommodation allowed by one policy is canceled out by the mandates (or interpretation of the mandates) of another. In addition, accommodations allowed or created by previous policy actors have been nullified by current policy actors based on their own interpretation and implementation of these intersecting policies. Furthermore, new accommodations have been created that may be more beneficial to the policy actors themselves than to the ELL students. (pp. 2–3)

But the notion of "one policy canceled out by the mandates of another" is not merely between policy makers and practitioners. The repercussions have serious implications for those engaged in teaching and learning and exemplify yet another case of failure in bridging the theory, practice, and policy gap. Wright (2005) sums up that disconnect in rather dismal terms:

The dramatic changes in the AZ LEARNS accountability formula—in which the exclusion of ELL scores plays a key role—resulted in a much rosier picture of education in Arizona. Besides a less embarrassing number of "Underperforming" schools that the state has to pay money to assist, there is one other important benefit. The elimination of bilingual education (and ESL), the imposition of the ill-defined SEI model, and the efforts to legally legitimize the placing of ELL students in mainstream classrooms will have a negative impact on the academic achievement of ELL students. The exclusion of ELL scores from the accountability program will help mask this failure. In other words, the negative impact of the ADE's (Arizona Department of Education) current policies will not (immediately) be reflected in a school's test scores or label. Thus, current ADE leaders can point to rising (aggregate) test scores and schools with impressive-sounding labels, and declare these proof that their restricted-oriented policies are improving the education of ELL students.

Under the current accountability system, it may take years before the harm that is being done to ELL students, especially in the primary grades of elementary school, will become evident. By then, current ADE leaders will no longer be in office, perhaps using the illusion of success to further their political careers. (p. 19)

In the case of the judicial battle between the Pinellas County school system and the federal court, there is an implicit notion that bridging the theory, practice, and policy gap is not without compromise, resulting in an implicit acknowledgement of the mismatch among theory, practice, and policy, albeit in political subtleties:

> That the first major court challenges to NCLB should arise over desegregation in southern systems is revealing about how dramatically federal priorities have shifted during the George W. Bush administration. The political and regulatory stance that the Education Department has taken is that local educational agencies must petition their judges for changes to court orders to comply with choice. . . . The relevant point about the federal implementation of NCLB is that in spite of its rhetoric, the federal Department is actually accommodating state and local demands. The Education Department has gradually softened its stance and is attempting to avoid high-profile conflicts, even if it does so tacitly and without official written approval. (DeBray, 2005, p. 183)

The schizophrenic role of the federal government as policy maker and translation of its policies into practices undergirded by theory is not only evident in its attempt to address the issues of congruency in closing the achievement gap between high- and low-performing students and children from disadvantaged and minority populations by demanding greater accountability in students' academic performance measured largely by high-stakes testing. It is also evident that there is a mismatch between its intent on ensuring that all children are taught by "highly qualified teachers," a notion coined by the federal agency that is rather limited in scope.

> In NCLB, the primary policy instrument through which federal lawmakers plan to improve teacher quality is requiring the demonstration of subject area knowledge. To be highly qualified, a teacher must have a bachelor's degree, be fully certified or licensed, and demonstrate competence in the subjects he or she teaches. A paraprofessional must possess 2 or more years of postsecondary education or pass a state test. As such, the teacher-quality provisions within NCLB intimate that certification, a college degree, and subject matter competence will translate to higher student achievement. (Cohen-Vogel, 2005, p. 32)

The myopia that underlies the attempt to align policy with practices for achieving excellence in teaching and learning is not only manifest in the extremely limited potency or manifest impotency of the federal agency to fully implement its policy but also the problematic it creates primarily for closing the achievement gap between high-and low-performing students, youths from disadvantaged groups and minority populations, and those with special needs. First, Cohen-Vogel (2005) contends that

> Washington has little leverage to enforce the teacher quality requirements in NCLB at the state level. If, in combination with failing to demonstrate progress toward proficiency by all student subgroups on standardized tests, the state educational agency fails to meet its teacher quality targets, the U.S. Department of Education can withhold federal funds dedicated to state administrative functions, but the amount is relatively insignificant (i.e., up to 1 percent of Title I allocations). If the department determines that a state continues to be out of compliance with the act's provision, it can make broader cuts in a state's federal funding. However, because most of these funds are dedicated to disadvantaged children and students with disabilities, deeper cuts may be viewed as "politically risky" by elected officials in Washington. (p. 33)

But the federal government's lack of "teeth" in enforcing sanctions against those school districts that fail to provide "highly qualified teachers" is but one side of the equation. The other side of the equation is even more dismal and provides a great deal of transparency to the inability of bridging the theory, practice, and policy gap for achieving excellence in teaching and learning—the shortage of teachers, particularly those who are "fully certified or licensed, and demonstrate competence," who are in special education, and who are in rural and urban school districts.

There is significant body of literature (Darling-Hammond, 1999, 2001, 2003; Darling-Hammond and Youngs, 2002; Ehrenberg and Brewer, 1994; Haberman, 1986; Haberman and Post, 1998; Irvine, 1990, 1997, 2002, 2003; Irvine and Armento, 2001; Ladson-Billings, 1994; et al.) that substantially makes the case for a significant positive relationship between the quality of classroom teachers and the anticipated academic achievement of the students who are present in those classrooms. The NCLB Act (NCLB, P.L. 107–110, 2001) recognizes that link between theory, practice, and policy, but what it seemingly fails to acknowledge is the shortage of teachers, particularly those who appear to be the focal point of the NCLB Act (NCLB, P.L. 107–110, 2001)—high- and low-performing students, children from disadvantaged and minority populations, and those with special needs.

Additionally, the creators of the NCLB seem to not only be oblivious to such shortages but feel that by merely waving the wand of legislative authority "with all deliberate speed" they can somehow reify the expectations of the act (NCLB, P.L. 107–110, 2001). Accordingly, Section 119 (qualifications for teachers and paraprofessionals) stipulates that the measurable objectives for achieving such expectations would

(1) IN GENERAL—Beginning with the first day of the first school year after the date of enactment of the No Child Left Behind Act of 2001, each local educational agency receiving assistance under this part shall ensure that all teachers hired after such day and teaching in a program supported with funds under this part are highly qualified.

(2) STATE PLAN—As part of the plan described in section 1111, each State educational agency receiving assistance under this part shall develop a plan to ensure that all teachers teaching in core academic subjects within the State are highly qualified not later than the end of the 2005–2006 school year. (NCLB, P.L 107–110, 2001)

The urgency of meeting the objectives certainly seems to ignore the persistent problem of teacher shortages as is clearly articulated by Howard (2003):

Although suburban and rural schools have encountered varying degrees of teacher shortages, much of the research on the topic has revealed that urban schools, typically in low income areas, experience higher degrees of teacher turnover and, as a result, greater teacher shortages than any other type of school. Thus, urban schools where many students are perennial underachievers, lack the most essential resource to overcome academic underachievement: a full array of qualified teachers. Because of the current dearth of teachers, students in urban and low-income areas are more likely than any other group of students to come into contact with underprepared and noncertified teachers, . . . [As well as] shortages . . . more pervasive in math and science, subjects in which students already lag far behind their suburban counterparts. . . [And] shortages . . . in bilingual and ESL classes, as well as in special education classrooms. (p. 143)

While there is an inordinate and even disproportionately greater emphasis and research on the shortages of "highly qualified" teachers in the urban areas, there is nevertheless a fairly substantial body of literature (Brownell, Bishop, and Sindelar, 2005; Brownell, Hirsh, and Seo, 2004; Collins, 1999; Kossar, Mitchem, and Ludlow, 2005; McLeskey, Tyler, and Flippin, 2004; National Rural Education Association (NREA), 2004; Reeves, 2002; Rosenkoetter, Irwin, and Saceda, 2004; Ryan, 1999; Schwartzbeck and Prince, 2003; Southeast Center for Teaching Quality, 2002; University of Washington, 2004; et al.) that documents the same kind of teacher shortages in the rural areas particularly among those responsible for teaching special education populations. Brownell, Bishop, and Sindelar (2005) describe the situation aptly:

> the "one size fits all" design is problematic, particularly for special education, whose shortage problem fails to match the NCLB solution of streamlined training for individuals with content expertise, and even more for rural special education where the availability of specialized content and Special Education teachers is even less viable. With the requirement to staff every classroom with a highly qualified teacher looming in the distant future, special education teacher qualifications are unclear, particularly for teachers who serve students with disabilities in multiple core subject areas. (p. 9)

## CONCLUSION

As dismal as the foregoing discourse may seem, there is much hope that there may yet be some attempts by various sectors within the sphere of schooling that recognize the need to address the structural impediments to bridging the theory, practice, and policy gap for achieving excellence in teaching and learning. Despite their lack of emphasis of integrating real community experiences, particularly for preservice teacher education candidates, the recent works by Darling-Hammond, Bransford, LePage, Hammerness, and Duffy (2005), Snow, Griffin, and Burns (2005) under the aegis of the National Academy of Education, and Comer (2004) come close to narrowing the theory, practice, and policy gap for achieving excellence in teaching and learning. Calculated reactions to NCLB may be the catalyst for ensuring that the gap is finally obliterated.

## REFERENCES

Bowles, S., Gintis, H., and Groves, M. O. (2005). *Unequal chances: Family background and economic success*. Princeton, NJ: Princeton University Press.

Brownell, M. T., Bishop, A. M., and Sindelar, P. T. (2005). "NCLB and the demand for highly qualified teachers: Challenges and solutions for rural schools." *Rural Special Education Quarterly, 24*(1), 9–15.

Brownell, M. T., Hirsh, E., and Seo, S. (2004). "Meeting the demand for highly qualified special education teachers during severe shortages: What should policy makers consider?" *The Journal of Special Education, 38*(1), 56–61.

Carnoy, M. (1974). *Education as cultural imperialism*. New York: David McKay.

Carnoy, M., Jacobsen, R., and Mishel, L. (2005). *The charter school dust-up: Examining the evidence on enrollment and achievement*. New York: Teachers College Press.

Cohen-Vogel, L. (January/March, 2005). "Federal role in teacher quality: 'Redefinition' or policy alignment?" *Educational Policy, 91*(1), 18–43.

Collins, T. (1999). "Attracting and retaining teachers in rural areas." Retrieved December 12, 2005, from ERIC Clearing House on Rural Education and Small Schools: http://www.acclaim-math.org/docs/htmlpages/Attracting%20and%20Retaining%20Teachers.htm.

Comer, J. P. (2004). *Leave no child behind: Preparing today's youth for tomorrow's world.* New Haven, CT: Yale University Press.

Darling-Hammond, L. (1999). *Teacher quality and student achievement: A review of state policy evidence.* Seattle: University of Washington, Center for the Study of Teacher Policy.

Darling-Hammond, L. (2001). The challenge of staffing our schools. *Educational Leadership, 58*(8), 12–17.

Darling-Hammond, L. (2003). "Keeping good teachers: Why it matters, what leaders can do." *Educational Leadership, 60*(8), 6–13.

Darling-Hammond, L., Bransford, J., LePage, P., Hammerness, K., and Duffy, H. (2005). *Preparing teachers for a changing world: What teachers should learn and be able to do.* San Francisco: Jossey-Bass.

Darling-Hammond, L., and Youngs, P. (2002). "Defining 'highly qualified teacher': What does 'scientifically-based research' actually tell us?" *Educational Researcher, 31*(9), 13–25.

DeBray, E. H. (2005). "NCLB accountability collides with court-ordered desegregation: The case of Pinellas County, Florida." *Peabody Journal of Education, 80*(2), 170–88.

Delpit, L., and Kilgour Dowdy, J. (Eds.). (2003). *The skin that we speak: Thoughts on language and culture in the classroom.* New York: New Press.

Ehrenberg, R. G., and Brewer, D. J. (1994). "Do school and teacher characteristics matter? Evidence from high school and beyond." *Economics of Education Review, 13,* 1–17.

Fischman, G. E., McLaren, P., Sünker, H., and Lankshear, C. (Eds.). (2004). *Critical theories, radical pedagogies, and global conflicts.* Lanham, MD: Rowman & Littlefield.

Foster, P. (1968). *Education and social change in Ghana.* Chicago, IL: University of Chicago Press.

Gay, G. (2000). *Culturally responsive teaching: Theory, research, and practice.* New York: Teachers College Press.

Gordon, J. A. (2000). *The color of teaching.* New York: Routledge/Falmer.

Greenberger, S. D. (2005). "Enforceable rights, No Child Left Behind, and political patriotism: A case for open-minded Section 1983 jurisprudence." *University of Pennsylvania Law Review, 153*(1011), 1011–56.

Haberman, M. (1986). "Alternative teacher certification programs." *Action in Teacher Education, 8*(2), 13–18.

Haberman, M., and Post, L. (1998). "Teachers for multicultural schools: The power of selection." *Theory into Practice, 37*(2), 96–104.

Howard, T. C. (Winter 2003). "Who receives the short end of the shortage? Implications of the U.S. teacher shortage on urban schools." *Journal of Curriculum and Supervision, 18*(2), 142–60.

Irvine, J. J. (1990). *Black students and school failure.* Westport, CT: Greenwood Press.

Irvine, J. J. (1997). *Critical knowledge for teachers of diverse learners.* Washington, D.C.: AACTE.

Irvine, J. J. (2002). *In search of wholeness: African American teachers and their culturally specific classroom practices.* New York: Palgrave/St. Martin's Press.

Irvine, J. J. (2003). *Educating teachers for a diverse society: Seeing with the cultural eye.* New York: Teachers College Press.

Irvine, J. J., and Armento, B. (Eds.). (2001). *Culturally responsive teaching: Lesson planning for elementary and middle grades.* Boston: McGraw-Hill.

Kossar, K., Mitchem, K., and Ludlow, B. (2005). "No Child Left Behind: A national study of its impact on special education in rural schools." *Rural Special Education Quarterly, 24*(1), 3–8.

Ladson-Billings, G. (1994). *The dreamkeepers: Successful teachers of African American children.* San Francisco: Jossey Bass.

Mattai, P. R. (1992). "Rethinking multicultural education: Has it lost its focus or is it being misused?" *Journal of Negro Education, 61*(1), 65–77.

McLeskey, J., Tyler, N. C., and Flippin, S. S. (2004). "The supply of and demand for special education teachers: A review of research regarding the chronic shortage of special education teachers." *The Journal of Special Education, 38*(1), 5–21.

National Rural Education Association. (2004). "Raising the alarm: Critical issues in rural education (Position Paper 1)." Retrieved December 12, 2005, from www.nrea.net/awards%20&%20other/NREA%20Position%20Paper%20I.doc.

Nieto, S. (1999). *The light in their eyes: Creating multicultural learning communities.* New York: Teachers College Press.

No Child Left Behind Act of 2001, Pub. L. No. 107–110, 115 Stat. 1425 (2002) (codified at 20 U.S.C. #6301-7941 [Supp. 1 2001]).

Orfield, G., and Kurlaender, M. (Eds.). (2001). *Diversity challenged: Evidence on the impact of affirmative action.* Cambridge, MA: Harvard Education Publishing Group.

Reeves, C. (2002). *Implementing the No Child Left Behind Act: Implications for rural schools and districts.* Napersville, IL: North Central Regional.

Rosenkoetter, S. E., Irwin, J. D., and Saceda, R. G. (2004). "Addressing personnel needs for rural areas." *Teacher Education and Special Education, 27*(3), 276–91.

Ryan, S. (1999). "Alaska's rural early intervention preservice training program." *Rural Special Education Quarterly, 18*(3/4), 21–28.

Schwartzbeck, T. T., and Prince, C. D. (2003). "How are rural districts meeting the teacher quality requirements of No Child Left Behind." Charleston, VA: Appalachia Educational Laboratory. Retrieved December 12, 2005, from www.ael.org/snaps/aasa-aelreport4.pdf.

Simpson, R. L., LaCava, P. G., and Graner, P. S. (November 2004). "The No Child Left Behind Act: Challenges and implications for educators." *Intervention in School and Clinic, 40*(2), 67–75.

Snow, C. E., Griffin, P., and Burns, M. S. (2005). *Knowledge to support the teaching of reading: Preparing teachers for a changing world.* San Francisco: Jossey-Bass.

Southeast Center for Teaching Quality. (2002). *Recruiting teachers for hard-to-staff schools: Solutions for the Southeast and the nation.* Chapel Hill, NC: Southeast Center for Teacher

Quality. Retrieved December 12, 2005, from www.teachingquality.org/resources/ SECTQpublications/Recruitment&RetentionStrategies.pdf.

Spring, J. (2005). *Political agendas for education: From the religious right to the Green Party* (3rd ed.). Mahwah, NJ: Lawrence Erlbaum Associates.

University of Washington. (October 2004). *Teacher turnover, teacher shortages, and the organization of schools.* Retrieved on December 12, 2005, from the Center for the Study of Teaching Policy Website: http://depts.washington.edu/ctpmail/PDFs/Turnover-Ing-01-2001.pdf.

Wright, W. E. (Spring 2005). "English language learners left behind in Arizona: The nullification of accommodation in the intersection of federal and state policies."*Bilingual Research Journal, 29*(1), 1–29.

# ODES: A Strategy for Effective Teaching and Learning in the Classroom

*Adnan Salhi*

## INTRODUCTION

*H*igh literacy manifests itself in the classrooms in several ways. High literacy appears when students are "engaged with literature, practiced in writing, comfortable with intelligent literacy discourse" (Langer, 2002, p. 1). Effective teachers help their students reach high levels of literacy by using effective strategies. ODES (Observe, Describe, Elaborate, and Share) is one of the strategies that, if implemented correctly, can help in bringing students to high levels of literacy. I developed this strategy when I was teaching creative writing and I used it in math, science, and language arts. ODES is very simple, easy to use, and my students always loved this strategy and repeatedly asked me to use it.

## INTRODUCING ODES STRATEGY

ODES has four phases and eleven steps. The phases and steps of this strategy are the following:

### Observe

*Step One*    Ask students to think carefully about one thing they learned or remember from the lesson/chapter they have finished. It can be a character in story, an idea in a math lesson, or a compound in a chemistry chapter, etc. Allow three to five minutes for students to identify their choices without telling anyone in the class what it is.

*Step Two*   Without any talking, have the students study what they thought of carefully and notice details about it. Tell the students to think about what they thought of and focus on the purpose, the structure, and the qualities of what they thought of.

## Describe

*Step Three*   Without writing down the name of what they thought of, have the students think of five to ten different words that describe what they thought of, its purpose, and the qualities that are unique to it. Have the students make a list of these five to ten words. This could be done with open texts or from memory with the textbooks closed.

## Elaborate

*Step Four*   Next, using the list of words the student created, have them use each word in a sentence.

*Step Five*   Once that task is completed, have the students take the list of sentences and create a poem that describes their object.

## Share

*Step Six*   After the students have created their poems, tell the students that they will now be sharing their poems. The rules for sharing their poems are below:

- Be patient and be respectful.
- Be a good listener and listen for details.
- You cannot ask the author of the poem questions.
- If you guess what the poem is about, do not shout out your guesses. You will be given time to share your guesses.
- When discussing guesses with your partners, do so in low voices.

*Step Seven*   Once you have gone over the rules for sharing, ask for volunteers to begin sharing their poems. Have the author read the poem carefully and clearly. The poem may need to be read more than once.

*Step Eight*   After each poem is read aloud, have the students silently guess what the poem described. They can either write down their guesses or remember them.

*Step Nine*   Have each student pair up with someone next to him/her and share their guesses, explaining the justification for this particular guess. Give the students one to two minutes to share their guesses. As a class, have the students share their guesses. Remind the author to try not to show expressions that will let the class know if they are right or wrong. Tell them that this increases the suspense and makes the activity more fun.

*Step Ten* Once every group has had a chance to share their guesses, have the author of the poem reveal what the poem described.

*Step Eleven* Repeat the procedures for sharing with everyone in the class.

## HOW DOES ODES FIT IN LITERACY THEORY AND RESEARCH?

The following pages provide a research and theory basis for each phase and step in ODES. In addition to doing the right things, it is very important for effective teachers to know why they do what they do. This knowledge opens wider windows for professional growth for teachers and literacy development for all students.

### Observing Phase

This phase covers the first two steps of the strategy. Each of these steps has its instructional goals and learning outcomes.

*Step One* When you ask your students to think of one thing they learned in a lesson you taught them, you are actually activating and assessing students' prior knowledge. This is important for several reasons.

In this step, students are asked to recall something that they have already learned. According to the schema theory, for readers to comprehend, they need experiences that will allow them to retrieve knowledge that they already have and build upon (Rumelhart, 1981). To retrieve prior knowledge and build on it, readers must select a useful schema from their "file" of prior knowledge. Being able to choose a desired schema is one of the principles of proficient reading (Gillet, Temple, Crawford, and Cooney, 2003).

This step also allows the students to choose a piece of information that perhaps they found particularly interesting or relevant. This gives the students a certain degree of "agency" or freedom that improves student interest in literacy activities (Greenleaf, Schoenbach, Cziko, and Mueller, 2001). Interest is integral to reading engagement. According to Greenleaf et al. (2001), reading engagement is one of the four components of literacy besides reading the words, mastering messages, and making meaning. Guthrie and Wigfield (1997) have also emphasized that the more engagement a reader has with a reading task, the more likely proficient reading will happen.

*Step Two* Without telling anyone in the class what each thought of, the teacher will have students think carefully about the topic, object, character, or event they thought of. The teacher will also instruct students to look for things that the ordinary person might miss about what they chose. Additionally, the teacher will allow five to seven minutes for students to decide on their choices and tell them to focus on the functions, the structure, qualities, or anything special about their topic of choice. This is significant for training students to become strategic learners.

As students search the text for important details, they begin creating connections between what they already know and what they are reading. This opportunity is important to reading comprehension. The schema theory also supports the idea that effective learning allows students to combine new and old information as well as seek out relationships between words and ideas.

This step also challenges students to decide what will be useful to their task and what will not. According to the schema theory, being able to use a schema to separate relevant information from information that is irrelevant is part of being a proficient reader (Anderson, 1985). It is important to notice, as Anderson and Pearson (1984) say, that readers may distort the text during this process by omitting or slightly changing details to fit their schemas. These changes and omissions will be corrected as in the following steps.

Challenging students to find what others might not have noticed will build their interest in reading. This also helps students pay attentions to details. According to Gillet et al. (2003), effective instruction for literacy learning should build skills as well as wills to read. The challenge of finding details that others might miss pushes students to read to learn, which, according to Gillet et al. (2003), is an important stage of reading development.

*Describing Phase*

*Step Three*    Without writing down the name of what they have chosen, the teacher will have students find five to ten words to describe their choice, its purpose, its function, or the qualities that are unique to it. This is done because it helps in students' literacy developments in many ways. Among these ways are the following:

Beginning with this step, students are now starting to write down words that pertain directly to their choice. This helps in students' vocabulary development. As Stahl (1999) says, readers need multiple exposures to new words before they truly learn them. As students search the text to find something unique to their choice, students will have a feel for the situation in which the word is used. This feel could not be obtained from a dictionary or a thesaurus.

This step helps students develop their communicative competence, which involves both the ability to produce a wide range of language forms, productive competence, and the knowledge needed to understand messages from a variety of sources, receptive competence (Harris and Hodges, 1995).

*Elaborating Phase*

*Step Four*   After constructing a list of words that are related to what they have chosen, the students use each word in a phrase or a sentence. This step helps students develop their reading maturity in the following ways:

Being able to expand upon the words that they have written by putting them into sentences or phrases shows students that they understand the word. Every student has four different types of vocabulary. One of these is written vocabulary. Written vocabulary is a person's ability to use a word correctly in writing. The ability to use a word correctly is a crucial part to students "knowing" a word (Rycik and Irvin, 2005).

This step also allows students to use and develop their syntactic knowledge as they consider the "rules" of how sentences are put together. In reading, according to Weaver (1988), "our intuitive knowledge of syntax, our grammatical schema, enables us to use word endings, functions words, and word order as cues to word identification" (p. 95).

*Step Five*   Once the task of putting the words in phrases and sentences is completed, the teacher asks the students to take the list of sentences and create an ode (poem) that describes their choice. The benefits of doing this to students' literacy development are numerous for several reasons.

At this point, teachers may suggest that students organize their phrases by their relationship to one another. According to the National Reading Panel (2000), helping students to connect and organize their ideas leads to 'better comprehension and achievement in social studies and science content areas" (p. 5). The schema theory also suggests that seeing the relationships among ideas is required in order to remember and comprehend (Alvermann, 1986).

Readers are most effective when they are able to see how each part of a text is related to its overall purpose (Luke and Freebody, 1999). When students compose a poem that describes a topic of their own choice as a result of ODES, students improve their communicative competence in an authentic way. When reading and writing activities are performed for real purposes, they are said to be "authentic" (Smith, 1982).

*Sharing Phase*

*Step Six*   After the students have created their poems, the teacher tells them that they will be sharing their poems based on the following rules:

• Be a good listener and pay attention to details.

- Don't ask the author of the poem any questions.
- As the authors read their odes/poems, try to guess what the poem describes.
- Be patient and don't shout out the answer because you will be given time to share your guess.
- Discuss your guess with a partner, and when you are discussing with your partners, do so in a low voice.

This step helps increase students' comprehension skills and reading proficiency in many ways. All students need to feel safe in order to participate. This is especially important for English language learners who, according to Herrell and Jordan (2004), need opportunities for both basic interpersonal communication and more cognitively demanding academic tasks.

Paying attention and listening to the poems each student reads and trying to guess what it describes provides a challenging task that is accomplished in a safe and secure environment. Students need "the opportunity to learn literacy through experiences that provide both challenge and security" (Rycik and Irvin, 2005, p. 7).

*Step Seven*    By going over the rules for sharing, asking for volunteers to begin sharing their poems, and having authors read their poems carefully and clearly more than once if needed, the teacher will be doing important parts of what effective literacy teachers do to provide balanced literacy for their students.

In the standards for English language arts of the National Council of Teachers of English, one principle says that "language arts learning activities are seldom discrete—'just reading,' 'just writing,' or 'just viewing,' for example. Each medium relates directly or indirectly to every other" (National Council of the Teachers of English & International Reading Association, 1996, p. 6). When students are reading, listening, thinking, and explaining their answers, they are immersed in a balanced literacy that includes opportunities for students to practice and improve their oral skills as well as their written and literacy skills.

This part gives students a chance to genuinely communicate with other students. This is important because "Students cannot develop communicative competence if the reading and writing they are doing does not genuinely communicate with anyone" (Rycik and Irvin, 2005, p. 58).

Allowing the students a chance to read their work to an audience gives them a sense of pride and responsibility. This feeling, ownership, is a major contributor to student interest in literacy activities because it allows readers to function as decision makers who choose the way of accomplishing their task and what to do when faced with a problem.

*Step Eight*   After each poem is read, have the students silently guess the answer to the riddle.

This step is asking all students in the class to make meaning from the poems being read. In order to do this, all students will have to recall a schema that is related to what is being read. After recalling their schemas, students will use it to build upon their prior knowledge as well as to create connections among new and old ideas. This process is beneficial in a reader's comprehension and retention (Anderson and Pearson, 1984).

*Step Nine*   When students pair up with someone near them and share their guesses explaining why they made that guess in one to two minutes and then share their guesses and explanations with the whole class, the teacher will be providing ample opportunities for social interactions between students. This setting is vital for learning for the following reasons:

The best literacy learning environments are highly social (Rycik and Irvin, 2005, p. 14) and provide numerous opportunities for verbal interactions that benefit all students including English language learners (Herrell and Jordan, 2004). Gillet and Temple (1994) support this idea by recommending that students have regular opportunities to read and participate in group discussions that allow them to compare their ideas to those of others.

Since there are no "wrong" answers as long as they can be explained and supported, this step allows a high degree of participation. For this same reason, students will build a great deal of confidence because they feel successful. According to Wigfield (1997), knowing that they can succeed is the first step in literacy engagement and motivation.

This step allows students to build and test their receptive competence as they work to interpret and understand the messages of a variety of individuals in their class (Rycik and Irvin, 2005).

Furthermore, by asking students to explain and support their guesses in reference to the text and to think critically about their partner's responses, this step guides students toward what Gillet et al. (2003) identify as the Mature Reading stage of reading development.

*Step Ten*   After students share their guesses, the teacher asks the author to reveal his/her topic and explain how the poem described the topic. This step is important because by asking the readers to explain how they chose their words and support their choices with the use of the text, students are evaluating their own thinking. This is an important part of using metacognition, and it is crucial to a student's ability to comprehend text. Brown (1985) noticed that students who are able to reflect on their own thinking processes while reading are able to take more active control of their reading.

*Step Eleven*   Repeating the procedures for "share" with every poem in the class is an important measure to ensure equity and growth for all students in the class.

## OTHER BENEFITS

There are many more benefits for ODES strategy that I have not mentioned because they do not apply to a specific step in the strategy, but rather to the strategy as a whole. Examples of these benefits are below:

During this strategy, the teacher has several opportunities to observe student learning as well as their strengths and weaknesses. This is crucial to effective assessment that, according to the International Reading Association's (2003) standards, should be an ongoing process that helps teachers make decisions and helps learners see that they are making progress.

ODES accommodates differences by allowing students to work at their distinct levels of abilities, help peers, and learn from classmates of different levels. This allows students to become proficient readers and feel like proficient readers. This successful feeling is an intrinsic motivator for students, a motivator that will last a lifetime and not just until the flavor is gone (Gambrell and Marinak, 1997).

ODES acknowledges the important balance the students need between guidance and independence. This is extremely important to students in the middle grades that are experiencing dramatic changes in their literacy instruction (Rycik and Irvin, 2005).

Furthermore, the most powerful learning is learned through experiences in which reading and writing are combined.

## APPLICATION OF ODES IN A FOURTH GRADE CLASSROOM

After training teachers to use this strategy, I asked some of them if they used it in their classroom. Many of them did. I asked some to report to me on how they used it and give some samples of their students' work as a result of using this strategy. Here is what one teacher wrote:

I have actually used this strategy twice in my classroom. The first time I used it I asked students to pick an object from the classroom to describe. I chose the flag so that I could use it for modeling. I then asked them to write down 5 to 10 descriptions of that object. I challenged them to try to think of descriptions that others might not have noticed. Before they started, we made a list of 10 descriptive words for the flag together. I was amazed by how difficult this step was for my students. They naturally wanted to write sentences not words. They did great, but being so used to writing in complete sentences made this difficult.

I then asked them to use the list of words they wrote down and to write short sentences or phrases in a poem-like form. Again, I modeled this step using the 10 words we picked for the flag. Just having finished a long unit of poetry, I reminded them to use things like personification, simile, metaphor, onomatopoeia, etc. At this point, a few of my students used similes for every word, which was not my intention. I also had many students who started each line with *I*. I am red with . . . like a riddle.

Next, I went over the rules for sharing and chose a student to read his poem twice to the class. I asked the students to guess silently what the poet was describing. I then asked them to discuss with a partner what they think the object is and why. As a class I called on some students to share and support their guesses. After a few students shared their guesses, I allowed the poet to reveal what his poem was about and explain how his poem describes the topic. I then chose another poet to share a poem and continued this procedure. By this time, almost all the students in the classroom wanted to share theirs and they couldn't raise their hand high enough to be called on to guess and share their thoughts.

The second time I used this strategy, I asked the students to describe a character, setting, object, etc. from piece of literature we were reading. We had just finished the novel, and it was a great time for review. While my class and I enjoyed doing this strategy with an object from the classroom, we loved it when we applied it to our novel. I was amazed at the details that my 4th graders were able to pull from the book (some that I missed after reading it several times!) and the discussions they had when they were asked to support their thinking and relate it to the text.

For example, one of my students wrote the following:

> Calm when it wants
> Silent like someone sleeping
> Holds beauty
> Deep as space
> Black like the night sky
> Silky as the clouds in Heaven
> Reused a google of times
> Waves good-bye
> Reflecting everything it sees

From this poem, my class had an in-depth discussion on whether this poem was written about the lake in the novel or the spring water. They were sure it was water but not sure which one. A few students pointed out that the line deep as space would make it seem bigger than a spring. I also loved the fact that this student in particular used reading, writing, science, and math concepts in writing this poem.

Almost every student in my classroom wanted to share their poem with the class and they were really excited about what they had done. One of my students that has ADD and struggles in writing (he will be in special education for writing next year) couldn't wait to share with the class. All of my speech students wanted to read their poems. This is a great way to differentiate instruction, beneficial for all of my students.

This was also a great assessment tool for me to find out what I need to teach my students. I learned a lot through observing them in groups and listening to their ideas and discussions.

## REFERENCES

Alvermann, D. E. (1986). "Graphic organizers: Cuing devices for comprehending and remembering main ideas." In J. F. Baumann (Ed.), *Teaching main idea/comprehension* (pp. 210–26). Newark, DE: International Reading Association.

Anderson, R. C. (1985). "Role of reader's schema in comprehension, learning and memory." In H. Singer and R. B. Ruddell (Eds.), *Theoretical models and processes of reading* (3rd ed.; pp. 372–84). Newark, DE: International Reading Association.

Anderson, R. C., and Pearson, P. D. (1984). "A schema-theoretic view of reading comprehension." In P. D. Pearson (Ed.), *Handbook of reading research* (pp. 255–91). New York: Longman.

Brown, A. L. (1985). *Teaching students to think as they read: Implications for curriculum reform*. Paper commissioned by the American Educational Research Association Task Force on Excellence in Education, October 1984. [ED 273 567]

Gambrell, L. B., and Marinak, B. (1997). "Incentive and intrinsic motivation to read." In J. T. Guthrie and A. Wigfield (Eds.), *Reading engagement: Motivating readers through integrated instruction* (pp. 205–17). Newark, DE: International Reading Association.

Gillet, J. W., Temple, C., Crawford, A., and Cooney, B. (2003). *Understanding reading problems: Assessment and instruction* (5th ed.). Boston: Allyn and Bacon.

Gillet, J. W., and Temple, C. (1994). *Understanding reading problems: Assessment and instruction* (4th ed.). New York: Harper Collins.

Greenleaf, C., Schoenbach, R., Cziko, C., and Mueller, F. (2001). Apprenticing adolescent readers to academic literacy. *Harvard Educational Review, 71*(1), 79–129.

Guthrie, J. T., and Wigfield, A. (Eds.). (1997). *Reading engagement: Motivating readers through integrated instruction*. Newark, DE: International Reading Association.

Harris, T. L., and Hodges, R. E. (Eds.). (1995). *The literacy dictionary*. Newark, DE: International Reading Association.

Herrell, A. L., and Jordan, M. (2004). *Fifty strategies for teaching English language learners*. Columbus, OH: Prentice Hall.

International Reading Association (IRA). (1996). *Standards for the English language arts*. Newark, DE: Author.

International Reading Association (IRA). (2003). *Standards for reading professionals*. Newark, DE: Author.

Langer, J. A. (2002). *Effective literacy instruction*. Urbana, IL: National Council of Teachers of English.

Luke, A., and Freebody, P. (1999). "Media and cultural studies in Australia." *Journal of Adolescent and Adult Literacy, 42*(8), 622–26.

National Council of the Teachers of English & International Reading Association. (1996). *Standards for the English language arts.* Urbana, IL: Author.

National Reading Panel. (2000). *Teaching children how to read: An evidence-based assessment of the scientific research literature on reading and its implications for reading instruction.* Washington, DC: National Institutes of Health.

Rumelhart, D. E. (1981). "Schemata: The building of cognition." In J. T. Guthrie (Ed.), *Comprehension and teaching: Research reviews* (pp. 3–26). Newark, DE: International Reading Association.

Rumelhart, D. E. (1984). "Understanding understanding." In J. Flood (Ed.), *Understanding reading comprehension* (pp. 1–20). Newark, DE: International Reading Association.

Rycik, J. A., and Irvin, J. L. (2005). *Teaching reading in the middle grades: Understanding and supporting literacy development.* Boston: Pearson Allyn and Bacon.

Smith, F. (1982). *Writing and the writer.* New York: Holt, Rinehart and Winston.

Stahl, S. A. (1999). *Vocabulary development.* Cambridge, MA: Brookline Books.

Weaver, C. (1988). *Reading process and practice: From sociolinguistics to whole language.* Portsmouth, NH: Heinemann.

Wigfield, A. (1997). "Children's motivations for reading and reading engagement." In J. T. Guthrie and A. Wigfield (Eds.), *Reading engagement: Motivating readers through integrated instruction* (pp. 14–33). Newark, DE: International Reading Associaton.

# Online Incidental Learning and Instantaneous Information Sharing in Teacher Education

## Han Liu

*This study explores practical approaches that appropriately fit into the online learning environment where enormous learning resources and instantaneous communication capabilities inspire incidental learning and promote cooperative learning to a higher level for K–12 teacher education. The Online Incidental Learning and Instantaneous Information Sharing strategy is demonstrated with concrete examples in educational technology and methods related courses.*

## INTRODUCTION

The opposite of incidental learning is intentional learning, which usually happens with a certain purpose in the learner's mind and in a formal setting such as the classroom. So incidental learning is unintentional or unplanned learning taking place in locations unrelated to formal learning contexts (Marsick and Watkins, 1992). Sometimes it is labeled "accidental learning" (School and Cooper, 1983). Incidental learning occurs often in the workplace, in a residential workshop, on porch steps, during evening social activities, during meals, at the computer lab, and in people's rooms late at night (Lawrence, 2000). It occurs when using computers in the process of completing tasks (Baskett, 1993; Cahoon, 1995). Watching TV, shopping, and traveling are also effective channels for incidental learning. Rogers asserted (1997) this "natural" way of learning is situated, contextual, and social. He suggests that adult educators need to build on how individuals learn naturally and incidentally.

Incidental learning covers all disciplines of knowledge and serendipitously increases particular knowledge, skills, or understanding (Lankard, 1995). Everyone has the experience of incidental learning at different conscious levels. However, adult learners often do not distinguish between formally and incidentally acquired learning (Mealman, 1993) or prefer incidental learning opportunities to formal ones (Cahoon, 1995; Ross-Gordon and Dowling, 1995). Although incidental learning is often not recognized or labeled as learning by learners or others (Ross-Gordon and Dowling, 1995), learners and educators are all realizing the fact that "unintended consequences of a learning situation are often more important to the learner than the original objectives" (McFerrin, 1999). Research indicates that incidental learning can result in improved competence, changed attitudes, and growth in interpersonal skills, self-confidence, and self-awareness (McFerrin, 1999; Mealman, 1993; Ross-Gordon and Dowling, 1995).

## INCIDENTAL LEARNING IN THE ONLINE ENVIRONMENT

In traditional classroom learning and even in traditional computer-assisted learning sessions, intentional learning dominates. In the digital age today, the Internet provides enormous opportunities for incidental learning. It "could possibly be classified as one of the most powerful and important self-directed learning tools in existence" (Gray, 1999). Herrmann, Fox, and Boyd (2000) acknowledged that unintended learning outcomes could result from the use of technology within educational contexts. Demand for online learning opportunities may result in fragmentation of learning opportunities and delivery modes, where the autonomous learner chooses the learning experience that meets his or her needs (Downes, 2001).

There is a growing awareness among educators today that effective university teaching and learning extends far beyond the development of skills and knowledge in specific subject domains (Dearing Report, 1997). Due to the extremely rich information resources and instantaneous communication capabilities of the online learning environment, much incidental learning occurred in a degree program that was not attributed to the course content itself (Lawrence, 2000). Northcote and Kendle (2001) purport that much valuable learning, primarily unintended, can take place away from the formal calculated context of universities and learning institutions. By recognizing the existence of such incidental, accidental, and peripheral learning experiences, instructors may encourage students to extend their repertoire of learning skills within both informal and formal contexts. Such learning may be more motivational and enjoyable for students. It is worthwhile to consider such influences when optimizing any learning environment.

The benefits of online incidental learning are multifaceted. Participating in online networks in a more incidental, informal manner can allow students to develop many useful skills including database searching, information filtering, data storage and retrieval, critical analysis of resources, and effective online communication (Northcote and Kendle, 2001). The Internet supports learning that is constructivist in nature, which builds on prior knowledge (Wilson and Lowry, 2000). Incidental learning also occurs in online discussion. In a survey of online group discussion members, 29 percent said their learning from the discussion is incidental and 53 percent said they learn both incidentally and deliberately at different times (Collins and Berge, 1996).

Although there has been little theory developed that explains the use of the Internet in learning outside of formal courses (Boshier and Pisutova, 2002), some approaches have been developed and applied in fostering online incidental learning. King (1990) suggested that the process of constructing new knowledge or the process of transforming previous knowledge into new formats is actually enhanced through peer interaction online. When students collaborate online by using e-mail or bulletin boards, such environments create contexts that are conducive to the socio-cognitive development of knowledge to occur (Gallini and Zhang, 1997; Stock, 1998) and promote learning partnerships and peer tutoring opportunities as useful strategies to enhance greater academic understanding in adult learning environments (Bleed, 2000). Incidental learning was also fostered through small-group interaction, flexible course assignments, peer stories, application of learning in work and personal contexts, instructor-facilitated discussions, and applied research assignments (Mealman, 1993). Rieber (1991) found that students were better able to learn incidentally delivered material without sacrificing intentional learning when that material was presented in an animated display on a computer and was divided into chunks of textual and visual sequences. He also found that recall of incidental information was more robust for pictures than for words. Northcote and Kendle (2001) proposed how to make use of incidental learning by using the Internet through recreation programs.

Today, most teacher candidates and teacher educators have to plow through masses of information online on a daily basis. A new challenge for teacher educators now is how to help the twenty-first-century K–12 teachers empower themselves to take responsibilities for their own learning and to use the full potential of the online learning opportunities.

According to Baylor (2001), it is important to investigate what is learned through the online incidental learning process. What information is ascertained along the way? What features of the website contribute to incidental learning? How is the obtained information retained and shared in the process? The purpose of this study is to elicit responses from participants on what they learned incidentally online and how the "Online Incidental Learning and Instantaneous Information Sharing" model helped them familiarize themselves with Internet skill, gain content knowledge, and learn from peers. The Online Incidental Learning and Instantaneous Information Sharing model is intended to help teacher candidates form a new learning habit that makes better use of the Internet technology, which enables them to use the learning skills and experiences obtained from applying this model to train the next generation, who will be well adapted to the digital learning environment in the twenty-first century.

## DESIGN OF THE STUDY

*Introduction of Online Incidental Learning and Instantaneous Information Sharing Model*

Based on the analysis of benefits from online incidental learning, the researcher initiated the Online Incidental Learning and Instantaneous Information Sharing model in an attempt to help teacher candidates make full use of online learning opportunities and enhance cooperative learning. This model had been used and developed over three semesters, and it was implemented by an assignment "My Web-Learning of the Week" in a graduate educational technology course. This assignment consisted of three steps. First, participants recorded whatever they learned incidentally while they were working on the Internet for whatever purposes at whatever time during the week; secondly, they would instantaneously e-mail their findings with a brief introduction and comment to the whole class (usually about fifteen to seventeen students) and the instructor on the e-mail list from Blackboard. Each participant was required to e-mail at least one finding (the cap is three findings) in each week. The findings might be a website, a web page, an article, a plug-in, a useful software, etc., regardless of the relevance to the course subject. At the third step, participants were required to present their finding(s) before the class using the instructor's computer station with PowerPoint at the beginning of the class each week. They would briefly answer four questions during the presentation.

1. Why are you interested in what you incidentally found?
2. How did you find it?
3. How did you index the learning into your previous knowledge structure?
4. How are you going to use it in your teaching in the future?

The second question was the most important. Students were required to elaborate the procedure of the learning in context. They would explain in the way such as "I was doing . . . when I incidentally found that. . . ." They would talk about the search engines they used, why they selected that search engine, what keywords were used, and why they thought the information was useful and reliable. The instructor would make comments and offer directions during the presentation. The assignment started from the second week of every semester and continued for eight weeks. It was worth eight points (one point each week) on a one-hundred-point scale and was graded on participation.

*Participants*

This study involved fifty-four graduate students (distributed in three semesters) in K–12 teacher education programs with various majors and minors. The computer literacy pre-test indicated that some of them were quite savvy in Internet activities, while some were familiar with word processing programs but with limited ability to process information on the Internet.

*Data Collection*

The online incidental findings submitted with "My Web-Learning of the Week" were summed up from three consecutive semesters. The web-learning contents were coded into ten categories (see table 3.1).

**Table 3.1. Web-Learning Contents**

| # | Category | Examples |
|---|----------|----------|
| 1 | Government | Department of Education and education-related governmental agencies at different levels, such as Department of Labor, Environmental Protection Agency, etc. |
| 2 | Educational Organizations | ERIC, teacher's unions, libraries, education research centers, etc. |
| 3 | Instruction and Learning | Lesson plans, pedagogical theories, instructional strategies, learning modules, teaching aids, etc. |
| 4 | Learning Standards | National and state standards, subject area standards, assessment tools, etc. |
| 5 | Professional Development | Workshops, action research papers, conferences, grants, publications, etc. |
| 6 | Research | Online journals, online databases, sample research papers, templates, etc. |
| 7 | Learning Tools | Dictionaries, encyclopedia, e-book reader, graphic editor, free online conference tools, etc. |
| 8 | Supplementary Materials | Supplementary curriculum materials: text, picture, animation, movie, PowerPoint, etc. |
| 9 | Daily Life | Shopping information, driving directions, salary indexes, weight loss, diet, online chatting, etc. |
| 10 | Entertainment | Free online music, music download websites, movie rental websites, games, etc. |

The data were collected from the learning outcomes (see figure 3.1) and the responses to the survey (see table 3.2) from the participants who had completed this assignment. The learning outcomes were measured on learning items (such as a web link, an article, a free software, a lesson plan template, and a interesting game) that the fifty-four participants e-mailed to the class and instructor during the three semesters.

The survey for participants' responses was a pilot questionnaire (see appendix at end of chapter) with no reliability and validity test having been conducted yet. It was developed based on the experimenter's own online incidental learning experience and his close observations on online incidental learning incidents from students taking the graduate course of educational technology.

By the end of each semester, the survey was conducted to collect data with nine questions, which required an answer of agree, disagree, and I don't know, and a short paragraph of reflective comment (see table 3.2). The survey questionnaire was delivered to all participants after the assignment was completed. Fifty of the total fifty-four participants had taken the survey.

## FINDINGS AND DISCUSSION

The following figure (3.1) demonstrates the distribution of incidentally found information on the Internet by fifty-four participants in three consecutive semesters.

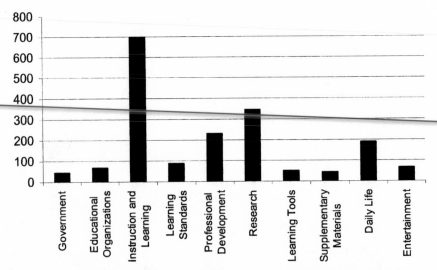

**Figure 3.1.   Distribution of Incidentally Found Information on the Internet (n=54)**

Since the participants were all in the teacher education program, it was reasonable that most of their online incidental learning was around themes of instruction strategies and learning theories. Next came research and professional development. Another finding is that they were interested in and had more opportunities to find information related to their daily lives, like finding a driving direction, downloading music, losing weight, and shopping, etc. The results could be interpreted that students tend to exert more efforts surfing on the Internet for their course-related learning purposes and daily life–related activities.

As to participants' responses to the assignment, both "numbers" and "words" were collected from fifty participants (93 percent of the participants) who responded to the surveys. Table 3.2 shows the results.

As table 3.2 shows, the quantitative part of the survey results reveal that the majority of the participants believe that the Online Incidental Learning and Instantaneous Information Sharing model helped them to learn online more effectively and efficiently in different learning areas. Based on the analysis of the

**Table 3.2.   Survey on My Web-Learning of the Week (n = 50)**

| # | Questions | Agree | Disagree | I Don't Know |
|---|-----------|-------|----------|--------------|
| 1 | This assignment helped me learn the necessary skills for processing information on the Internet. | 98% | 0% | 2% |
| 2 | This assignment helped me better understand the structure of the web pages and websites. | 75% | 13% | 12% |
| 3 | This assignment provided opportunities for me to learn from different cases that were authentic in real-life situations. | 81% | 12% | 7% |
| 4 | By completing this assignment, I learned a lot more than the course requirement and the textbook. | 77% | 11% | 12% |
| 5 | I learned a lot from my peers, both content and the way they learn incidentally on a daily basis. | 92% | 8% | 0% |
| 6 | The "Instantaneous Information Sharing" feature of this assignment enabled me to know how my classmates processed information online, and I could get further advice in a timely manner. | 86% | 4% | 10% |
| 7 | I was motivated by my peers' progress and the "Instantaneous Information Sharing" mechanism. | 77% | 12% | 11% |
| 8 | This is a tedious assignment. It is too easy for me. | 9% | 89% | 2% |

My comments on this assignment

"numbers" from the table and the "words" from the general reflective comments, three themes appeared.

*Theme One: The students gained more knowledge and skills than provided in the textbooks and lectures with concrete examples in the following areas.*

- Necessary skills in processing information on the Internet
- Higher level understanding of Internet structures in a holistic fashion
- Diversity of learning methods from peers
- Useful free software tools from each other.

Comments on the assignment from the survey corroborated these findings. Some of the comments are listed below. (The names appearing in the comments are all pseudonyms.)

- I learned a lot that is not in the textbook and in the teacher's syllabus.
- With the E-Book Reader that I learned from my peer, I can read on-line for free or at very low coast.
- The website www.brainpop.com Steve shared with us in class is really amazing. It covers all subject areas and with movies and interactive quizzes.
- I don't know the how to search images before Tony demonstrated how fast he could find desired images using the image search features of the search engine. When I want a picture I used to search on websites to find it. It takes a long time and oftentimes the finding is not ideal.
- Upon receiving the e-mail that has interactive geography quizzes, I exclaimed: "Aha, dear, that is really what I want."
- I didn't know we can use Google.com to search for driving directions until Janet told us. I thought mapquest.com is the only website for map search.
- Dictionary and encyclopedia such as http://www.acronymfinder.com/ and http://wikipedia.org/ are really good stuff. They are updated on-line reference tools offering very recent information.
- The site http://www.free-graphics.com/ is really amazing for me to download the animal pictures for my kindergarten teaching.
- When I was search for lesson plans I followed some of the links and grabbed many useful websites, and I book-marked them all as Samuel did.

*Theme two: The students adapted to learning cooperatively using technology that enables instantaneous communication.*

- I feel comfortable to ask my peers for an answer through e-mail if I have questions.

- Solomon became a teacher in the class. He knows many small programs that are easy to use, and most importantly it is free.
- Everyone can download and install by oneself.
- Do you remember the PowerPoint for the lesson plan? Roger helped me figure out how to integrate the movie.

*Theme Three: Students become more motivated and more comfortable in using the Internet as an incidental learning tool on a daily basis.*

- My interest in using computer as a powerful learning tool has increased dramatically with the practice in this assignment. We were competing with each other to show off our treasures hunted from the Internet even though the teacher said the grade for this assignment is based on participation.
- Surfing on the Internet is really fun and academically helpful, so long as you keep a keen eye and critical mind with each click of you mouse.
- Why not follow the links to the end? There might be treasures there!
- I become so engaged now when online. I used to feel boring with that many overwhelming information.

In summary, this assignment helped students learn the necessary online learning skills through concrete, individualized, and authentic incidental learning cases. The "instantaneous information sharing" feature of this assignment fostered cooperative learning, through which participants gained substantive knowledge and practical skills that the mandated courses and technical tutorials did not touch or elaborate. Much learning takes place informally and incidentally, beyond explicit teaching or the classroom. Faculty can enhance informal and incidental learning in specific ways. The following section explains other aspects of the whole story.

In the open-ended online learning environment, each individual student accesses information from different sources and using various technical skills. Every student, graduate student in particular, can be a very good teacher to his or her peers and to the instructor as well. Each individual's learning is unique both in contents and styles. This is totally different from the traditional way of learning with the same textbook from the same instructor, dictated by the same curriculum framework. In her online incidental learning presentation, one of the Internet-savvy students mentioned that she used a Boolean search for her complicated search objectives. The whole class was shocked with this powerful method of organizing keywords for complicated searching. No one had used that skill before. Recognizing that was a critical learning moment, the instructor let the student continue to lecture on her Boolean Search skills. The rest of that class was dedicated to efficient use of search engines.

The Online Incidental Learning and Instantaneous Information Sharing model creates a formidable learning momentum with immediate access of resources and instantaneous information sharing that did not exist before the digital age. There is a chain reaction after students share each other's incidental findings. They are eager to use what they have just learned to try another similar search or test with some variation in selecting search engines or redefining keywords. One student introduced to the class his online incidental learning: freeware that can change Word-format files into PDF format. The whole class was very excited about that software. They were all itching to try it at once. Since student computer stations in the computer lab were not allowed to install any software under the technology administration regulations, the instructor announced, "Go back home tonight and try this software in your home computer." The students looked very disappointed because their learning momentum was destroyed. This example demonstrated how important it is to keep learning momentum in a smooth flow of rapidity. Technology effectively accommodates learning momentums with its easy access and instantaneous communication capabilities. Rigid computer lab rules for graduate students hinder that momentum.

Another benefit of this assignment beyond the researcher's expectations that the students were fully engaged outside class. They did this assignment in a casual but engaging manner. Especially after the first few weeks, they had an attitude of inquiry and research, trying to find something unique to impress the class next week. So online incidental learning, if instantaneously shared with the whole class, can be a powerful intrinsic motivator for learning.

Given that this study was primarily exploratory in nature, these results should only be considered as preliminary.

## CONCLUSION

All though this study was conducted on teacher candidates, it also has implications for K–12 students who are also exposed to the Internet resources on a daily basis. Online Incidental Learning and Instantaneous Information Sharing is also a powerful learning tool for children. Nobody would deny that children up to the age of six are learning a lot incidentally. But at the age of six, incidental learning loses its importance and is replaced by a "sit down, listen and repeat" approach (Anderson, 1985). In the online environment, multimedia and hyperlinks play very important roles in motivating students to learn and enhance their memorization constructively. Multimedia elements received a higher level of acceptance than the classical education methods. Supported by carefully selected multimedia elements to serve as "anchor points" the learner builds a network of facts—a mind map of the knowledge contained in hypertext (Holzinger, Pichler, Almer, and Maurer, 2001). As the Internet becomes more a mainstay than blackboard and chalk in K–12 classrooms, an imperative demand for teacher educators appears even more salient: Get K–12 schools teachers well prepared for the paradigmatic change in instruction and learning in the twenty-first century.

The Internet has changed and is still changing human cognitive patterns and learning habits. People learn anytime, anywhere with easy Internet access in efficient and creative ways. The Online Incidental Learning and Instantaneous Information Sharing model extend learning opportunities and foster cooperative learning in an authentic, contextual, and constructivist manner. It is fun, engaging, motivational, and leads to well-indexed knowledge for online learners.

## REFERENCES

Anderson, J. R. (1985). *Cognitive psychology and its implications* (2nd ed.). New York: Freeman, 172–73.

Baskett, H. K. M. (1993). "Workplace factors which enhance self-directed learning." Paper presented to the Seventh International Symposium on Self-Directed Learning, West Palm Beach, FL, January 21–23 (ED 359 354).

Baylor, A. L. (2001). "Perceived disorientation and incidental learning in a Web-based environment: Internal and external factors." *Journal of Educational Multimedia and Hypermedia, 10*(3), 227–51.

Bleed, R. (2001). "A hybrid campus for the new millennium." *Educause Review, 36*(1), 16–24.

Boshier, R., and Pisutova, K. (2002). "Using the Internet for informal learning about joining the brain drain: A qualitative Central/East European and Pacific perspective." In J. Pettit et al. (Eds.), *Proceedings of the Adult Education Research Conference, North Carolina State University, Raleigh, NC, May 24th, 2002.* Raleigh: NCSU, 2002.

Cahoon, B. B. (1995). "Computer skill learning in the workplace: A comparative case study." Ph.D. diss., University of Georgia, 1995. Retrieved from www.arches.uga.edu/~cahoonb/dissertation.html.

Collins, M. P., and Berge, Z. L. (1996). "Mailing lists as a venue for adult learning." Paper presented at the Eastern Adult, Continuing and Distance Education Research Conference, University Park, PA, October 24–26, 1996. Retrieved on August 10, 2005, from www.emoderators.com/papers/EACDERC.html

Dearing Report. (1997). *Higher education in the learning society.* London: HMSO.

Downes, S. (2001). "The fragmentation of learning." *Education Canada, 41*(3), 4–7.

Gallini, J. K., and Zhang, Y. (1997). "Socio-cognitive constructs and characteristics of classroom communities: An exploration of relationships." *Journal of Educational Computing Research, 17*(4), 321–29.

Gray, D. E. (1999). "The Internet in lifelong learning: Liberation or alienation?" *International Journal of Lifelong Education, 18*(2).

Herrmann, A., Fox, R., and Boyd, A. (2000). "Unintended effects in using learning technologies." *New Directions for Adult and Continuing Education, 88,* 39–48.

Holzinger, A., Pichler, A., Almer, W., and Maurer, H. (2001). "TRIANGLE: A multimedia test-bed for examining incidental learning, motivation and the Tamagotchi-effect within a game-show like computer based learning module." Retrieved on October 1, 2005, from www.iicm.edu/iicm_papers/triangle.pdf.

King, A. (1990). "Enhancing peer interaction and learning in the classroom through reciprocal questioning." *American Educational Research Journal, 27,* 664–87.

Lankard, B. A. (1995). *New ways of learning in the workplace. ERIC Digest 161.* Columbus, OH: ERIC Clearinghouse.

Lawrence, R. L. (2000). "Transcending boundaries: Building community through residential adult learning." Chicago, IL: National-Louis University, 2000. Retrieved from www.nl.edu/ace/Resources/Documents/TranscendingBoundaries.html.

Marsick, V. J., and Watkins, K. E. (1992). "Informal and incidental learning in the Workplace" (book review). *Adult Education Quarterly, 42,* 194–95.

McFerrin, K. M. (1999). "Incidental learning in a higher education asynchronous online distance education course." In J. D. Price et al. (Eds.), *SITE 99: Society for Information Technology & Teacher Education International Conference Proceedings.* Charlottesville, VA: Association for the Advancement of Computing in Education (ED 432 288).

Mealman, C. A. (1993). "Incidental learning by adults in nontraditional degree program." In K. Freer and G. Dean (Eds.), *Proceedings of the 12th Annual Midwest Research-to-Practice Conference.* Columbus: Ohio State University (ED 362 663). Retrieved from www.nl.edu/ace/Resources/Documents/Incidental.html.

Northcote, M., and Kendle. A. (2001). "Informal online networks for learning: Making use of incidental learning through recreation." Paper presented at the International Education Research Conference, Fremantle, December 2–6, 2001. Retrieved August 1, 2005, from www.aare.edu.au/01pap/nor01596.htm

Rieber, L. P. (1991). Animation, incidental learning, and continuing motivation. *Journal of Educational Psychology, 83*(3), 318–28.

Rogers, A. (1997). "Learning: Can we change the discourse?" *Adults Learning 8*(5), 116–17.

Ross-Gordon, J. M., and Dowling, W. D. (1995). "Adult learning in the context of African-American women's voluntary organizations." *International Journal of Lifelong Education, 14*(4), 306–19.

School, B. A., and Cooper, A. (1983). "Incidental and accidental learning: Use them!" *Academic Therapy, 18,* 583–91.

Stock, R. (1998). "Teaching online communication skills: An activity using aspects." *English Journal, 87*(1), 63–66.

Wilson, B., and Lowry, M. (2000). "Constructivist learning on the web." *New Directions for Adult and Continuing Education, 88,* 79–88.

## APPENDIX: QUESTIONNAIRE FOR ASSIGNMENT:
## "MY WEB-LEARNING OF THE WEEK"

| # | Questions | Agree | Disagree | I Don't Know |
|---|-----------|-------|----------|--------------|
| 1 | This assignment helped me learn the necessary skills for processing information on the Internet. | | | |
| 2 | This assignment helped me better understand the structure of the web pages and websites. | | | |
| 3 | This assignment provided opportunities for me to learn from different cases that were authentic in real-life situations. | | | |
| 4 | By completing this assignment, I learned a lot more than the course requirement and the textbook. | | | |
| 5 | I learned a lot from my peers, both content and the way they learn incidentally on a daily basis. | | | |
| 6 | The "Instantaneous Information Sharing" feature of this assignment enabled me to know how my classmates processed information online, and I could get further advice in a timely manner. | | | |
| 7 | I was motivated by my peers' progress and the "Instantaneous Information Sharing" mechanism. | | | |
| 8 | This is a tedious assignment. It is too easy for me. | | | |

My comments on this assignment

# Strategies for Developing Collaborative Skills in Undergraduate and Graduate Teacher Education Programs

## *Karen Schulte*

*The research on student achievement and many school practices mandated by state and federal legislation provide evidence of the importance of adult collaboration to improve student learning. Historically, educators have not had the training nor seen the need to become skillful collaborators. As it becomes increasingly clear that current and future educators will need to bring strong collaborative skills to the school setting, it is imperative that teacher preparation programs, both on the undergraduate and graduate levels, develop strategies to foster such skills. This chapter presents a rationale for integrating collaborative skills into teacher education courses and describes a number of strategies used successfully in undergraduate and graduate teacher education courses to model, teach, and practice these skills.*

## INTRODUCTION

The National Staff Development Council (NSDC) recently revised its standards for quality professional development in K–12 schools (2001). The revisions were based on what we know about adult learning, personal and organizational change, and the variables that impact student achievement. Two of these standards are of particular importance when considering the need for collaborative skills among the adults in school settings:

- Staff development that improves the learning of all students organizes adults into learning communities whose goals are aligned with those of the school and district, and
- Staff development that improves the learning of all students provides educators with the knowledge and skills to collaborate. (NSDC, 2001)

In developing these standards, NSDC clearly recognized and affirmed the importance of collaborative skills among K–12 educators for improving student achievement.

This has not always been the case. Education is often viewed as a profession in which little interaction among adults is necessary. Teachers have almost complete autonomy in their classrooms, interacting to a much greater extent with their students than with other adults in their buildings. As this paradigm shifts, schools are having mixed success with collaborative change efforts, and adult relationships are often identified as significant obstacles to substantive improvement in student achievement.

## A RATIONALE FOR COLLABORATION IN SCHOOLS

There is a strong correlation between the trust evident in adult relationships in schools and improvement in student achievement (Byrk and Schneider, 2002). Relationships between teachers and students, teachers and other teachers, teachers and parents, and teachers and administrators are intricately linked, and schools function as successful organizations when there is synchrony within these various relationships. Byrk and Schneider (2002) define four criteria for developing trust in school relationships: respect, competence, personal regard for others, and integrity. They offer significant evidence linking relational trust to improvements in student learning, analyzing data from three Chicago schools reflecting both the change in trust levels (as reported by teachers) and the changes in student achievement in math and reading. They found that trusting relationships among the adults in a school setting encourage teachers to take risks, collaboratively problem-solve, and personally commit to the mission of their school and that these variables positively impact student achievement.

Barth (2004) lends his voice to this discussion by emphasizing the strong need for adult reflection in improving teachers' "craft knowledge" and the role that collaboration plays in supporting and extending this reflection. Reflecting on practice does not happen in isolation but rather as practice is discussed and dissected with colleagues. Principals are seen as vital in developing an adult community of learners in which frequent professional dialogue is the norm rather than the exception.

On a practical level, educators are being asked more than ever to collaborate effectively to improve student learning. Mandatory K–12 school improvement efforts have long recognized the importance of collaboration in analyzing data, determining improvement goals, and identifying effective strategies to improve student learning. Both school improvement legislation and the accreditation processes for K–12 schools have emphasized the importance of staff consensus and building-wide improvement efforts. Whole school reform is necessary to impact student learning. This requires serious and honest conversations among staff, something that does not come naturally in many schools and requires consistent and skillful collaboration.

Professional development efforts in K–12 schools have changed, recognizing that teacher buy-in is imperative for any change strategy to be effective in improving student achievement. Adult learning is no longer seen as an individual journey but rather as a collaborative group process. Collaborative modeling, observing, analyzing student work, developing lesson plans, reviewing and analyzing student achievement data, and co-teaching are becoming the hallmarks of improving schools. Principals and other school leaders struggle to create cultures of collaboration within their schools, often with little success. Teachers report frustration with the lack of time available to work together and the resources to support these efforts, obstacles often cited as preventing meaningful collaboration. When these obstacles are eliminated, however, it is still difficult for teachers to work together collaboratively, most having never had this opportunity and many lacking the necessary skills. No Child Left Behind lends a sense of urgency to these efforts. Adequate yearly progress for all students is monitored and evaluated. The stakes are high and the consequences are public.

Given strong evidence that today's teachers need to demonstrate effective collaborative skills, it is surprising that more is not done in teacher education programs on the undergraduate or graduate level to develop such skills. This is not only true explicitly, as evidenced by the scarcity of courses in teacher education programs focusing on developing collaborative skills, but it is also true implicitly, as evidenced by the scarcity of authentic modeling and opportunities to practice collaboration in many teacher education courses.

## COLLABORATIVE SKILLS: A FRAMEWORK

A framework for developing collaborative skills might include the following (Kampwirth, 2003):

- Interpersonal skills,
- Communication skills,
- Problem-solving skills,
- Organizational and teaming skills, and
- Self-reflection skills.

The challenge for teacher education programs is to integrate modeling and practice of these skills into both undergraduate and graduate courses. In addition to opportunities for students to observe and practice collaborative skills, these skills must also be defined and explained explicitly, and students must understand the rationale and need for these skills in today's schools.

## SOME SUGGESTED STRATEGIES

*Book Groups*

I use book groups regularly in courses I teach and have received very positive feedback from students. They often comment that it is the first time they have read a professional book and had an opportunity to discuss it with peers. Book groups may be integrated into both undergraduate and graduate level courses. I divide students into groups of four to five, and each group is either assigned or chooses from a menu of options a professional book to read and discuss over the course of a semester. I allocate time regularly for book groups to meet during class sessions. Roles within the group are assigned and rotated and usually include a facilitator, timekeeper, and recorder. Each group determines its own reading schedule, and the facilitator must come prepared to structure and lead the discussion for his or her assigned sessions. I model using key questions, controversial quotes, and personal experiences as ways to begin a discussion. I often require a product or presentation of some type as a culminating activity. In some cases, it is helpful to begin with shorter articles or chapters and then progress to reading and discussing books. It is necessary to teach and model the importance of the facilitator's role, and initially I find it helpful to structure some discussion questions for each group. I also find it useful, particularly with undergraduate students, to identify and define ground rules for discussions, often including active listening, coming prepared, demonstrating respect for ideas of others, and making sure everyone gets a chance to express opinions.

We take time at the end of each book group session to debrief how the process is going. I have used rating scales, journal writing, and suggestion box activities to surface any problems in the collaborative process that we need to talk about as a class. A particularly useful and open-ended way to check in is to ask students to do a five-minute quiet writing on these questions:

- What is working for you in your book club?
- What suggestions do you have that would make your book club a more meaningful experience?

We discuss responses to these questions as a class and relate our experiences to the collaborative skills needed by teachers. Many school staffs participate in book groups as a form of professional development, and preparing students for this type of activity, as well as fostering the habit of reading and discussing professional literature, is an important component of a teacher education program.

*Post-It Notebooks*

As undergraduate students begin to work in school settings as pre-student teachers or student teachers, they have many questions and there are few opportunities for discussing them with others. Students in graduate programs are often teaching and should be encouraged to use collaborative self-questioning and reflection as a normal part of their professional development. I have found a helpful strategy for both situations to be a post-it notebook. I ask students to purchase a spiral notebook and a package of post-it notes. Every time they have a question about something that happens in the classroom or in the larger school setting, I encourage them to write it on a post-it and stick it on a page in their notebook. We designate a portion of each class session to post-it notebook discussion. A specific format is followed for these discussions:

- Choose a post-it situation or question that you are interested in discussing.
- Read your post-it to your group.
- Group members ask clarifying questions.
- Group members make suggestions about ways to handle the situation in question while the reader jots down notes and ideas.
- The post-it reader states what he or she will do differently, based upon the suggestions received and creates a short action plan.
- During a later class session, people report in on their progress and successes.

Initially, I model this procedure for the whole class, but after two to three weeks, I divide the class into post-it groups of four to five students. They take turns being the post-it reader. During a twenty-minute period, following the procedure above (which does not allow discussion to veer off track), we can usually complete two post-it situation discussions.

This is an excellent activity for modeling and practicing collaborative problem solving. I have received positive feedback from students who have participated in this activity, particularly those who are student teaching at the time. It is important to adhere to the steps in the procedure, which purposely focus on a positive problem-solving model and keep the conversation focused on the topic. Some examples of issues we discussed using this technique in a recent student teaching seminar course are listed below:

- What is the best discipline method for middle school students with physical impairments?
- How do I deal with a teacher who makes little or no modifications or adaptations for students with disabilities?
- I have a few kids who are ninth graders who can't tell time. How do I help them learn?
- I have three students who have a love-hate relationship with each other. How do I get them to coexist in my classroom?
- How do I stop student tattling?

This activity not only teaches collaborative skills but also helps teachers and student teachers see that they are not the only ones experiencing difficulty. Once they learn that no teacher is perfect and that it is acceptable, even encouraged, to discuss problems with colleagues, the conversations tend to be very lively. It is rewarding to see their confidence grow as they learn that many of their suggestions had a positive impact.

*Vision Sharing Activities*

It is important for educators to have a personal vision for themselves and to be able to articulate and discuss this vision with colleagues. This forms the foundation for making sound instructional and classroom management decisions. Both the articulation and the sharing of one's vision can be difficult, however, and I find that this requires focused effort and modeling. I often start by asking students to draw pictures illustrating their visions of themselves as teachers. I then use graphic organizers to encourage students to become more specific about the attributes and behaviors they believe are important in a teacher. I then ask students to write about their visions of themselves as educators. We use the stages of process writing as we do this, enabling students to practice reading their papers to peers as they edit, revise, and extend their thinking. This process culminates in an "Author's Chair" activity in which each student reads his or her vision to two or three other students. As a group, they discuss the commonalities of their visions and how these commonalities contribute to the collective vision of education.

This activity was particularly helpful in a graduate-level course I recently taught on language arts strategies for students with disabilities. Students created a vision of the language arts program they wanted to establish in their classrooms. They struggled with this at first, but the feedback on the final products was very positive. One student reported that she shared her vision with her building principal and, as a result, received funding for additional professional development and resources to support her efforts.

## Goal Cards

I often ask graduate students who are currently teaching and student teachers to fill out a goal card at the beginning of the semester, identifying their one or two professional goals for that semester and developing an action plan for reaching these goals. We share them as a class and periodically report in on our progress. Collaborative skills are reinforced as we discuss successes, failures, and frustrations and problem-solve together. Examples of recent goals student teachers established for themselves are below:

- To teach Christopher (a student with severe disabilities) to take his coat off in under twenty-five minutes.
- To improve my behavior management skills.
- To work on developing effective time schedules for the classroom.
- To work on my own time-management skills.
- To learn everything I can about testing students for special education evaluations.

I always complete a goal card along with the students, modeling that improvement is a never-ending process.

## Cooperative Learning and Learning Clubs

I use a number of cooperative learning activities in my courses, and I make sure to define and discuss the collaborative skills needed for various activities. I often ask students to write reaction papers after such an activity, reflecting upon their use of collaborative skills and their contributions as group members. I ask them to focus on identifying some collaborative skills they would like to improve, and then we follow-up on these areas later in the semester.

I find it helpful for students to belong to a core group, which I call a learning club, so that they can truly get to know one another and develop close, collaborative relationships. I use a learning style inventory to divide them into their learning clubs so that each group represents a diversity of style. I also balance the groups in terms of race and gender. I never allow students to self-select groups, and we talk about the reasons this may not be an effective method for group formation. In the beginning of each semester, I structure a number of learning club activities so that group members get to know and trust each other. During the last class session, I always ask learning club members to write thank you notes to each other, identifying ways in which all group members contributed to the functioning of the group.

I have found using learning clubs to be an extremely valuable component of teaching collaborative skills. This process models being part of a team in the workplace, whether it is a grade-level team, a departmental team, a special education service delivery team, or any one of a variety of other teams to which teachers may belong. On a few occasions, I have had to deal with some group dynamic problems. This usually involves a student who is not attending class regularly or completing group tasks. Dealing with these issues with an entire team models the problem-solving and conflict resolution skills required to be a part of an effective team.

*Collaborative Skills Self-Assessment*

I regularly ask students to complete an assessment of their collaborative skills. I use a simple self-assessment instrument (see appendix at end of chapter) which may be modified to fit a variety of courses and student populations. After completing a self-assessment, I ask students to develop a collaboration skills profile, identifying their strengths and weaknesses and a self-improvement goal. As time permits, I ask students to review research related to their self-improvement goal and to develop an action plan for reaching this goal. Profiles, goals, and action plans are all shared with their peers and discussed regularly.

## CONCLUSION

It is clear that educators must demonstrate strong collaborative skills. It is not clear that all teachers entering the field have developed these skills. Efforts to improve student learning are dependent upon the adults in our schools working as a team, collaboratively striving to improve the educational experiences of their students. Collaborative problem solving, modeling, observing, analyzing student achievement data, developing effective lesson plans, and other practices are becoming the expected norm in many of our schools. Unfortunately, these often meet with little success if the adults are not able to work together effectively.

Teacher preparation programs must develop implicit and explicit strategies to foster collaborative skills in both our undergraduate and graduate students. Historically, this has not been a strong focus of many teacher preparation programs. The use of numerous classroom strategies to both model and provide practice in collaborative skills is of the utmost importance as we prepare our students to become the next generation of teachers.

# REFERENCES

Barth, R. (2004). *Learning by heart.* San Francisco: John Wiley and Sons.

Bryk, A. S., and Schneider, B. (2002). *Trust in schools: A core resource for improvement.* New York: Russell Sage Foundation.

DeBoer, A. (2000). *Working together: The art of consulting and communicating.* Longmont: Sopris West.

Kampwirth, T. (2003). *Collaborative consultation in the schools: Effective practices for students with learning and behavior problems.* Upper Saddle River: Merrill Prentice Hall.

National Staff Development Council. (2001). *Standards for staff development.* Retrieved July 5, 2005, from www.nsdc.org.

# APPENDIX: COLLABORATIVE SKILLS SELF-ASSESSMENT

Rate yourself in the following skill areas. A rating of 1 indicates lots of room for improvement; a rating of 5 indicates close to perfection.

## General Communication Skills

Paying attention to nonverbal communication of others (body language, eye contact, etc.)
1_____2_____3_____4_____5 Comments:
Using active listening skills (paraphrasing, summarizing, probing, etc.)
1_____2_____3_____4_____5 Comments:
Being empathic
1_____2_____3_____4_____5 Comments:
Being appropriately assertive
1_____2_____3_____4_____5 Comments:
Using questioning appropriately
1_____2_____3_____4_____5 Comments:
Using professional written communication skills
1_____2_____3_____4_____5 Comments:
Other:_____
1_____2_____3_____4_____5 Comments:

## General Organizational Skills

Being on time
1_____2_____3_____4_____5 Comments:
Meeting deadlines
1_____2_____3_____4_____5 Comments:

Keeping track of details
1_____2_____3_____4_____5  Comments:
Planning ahead and scheduling time appropriately
1_____2_____3_____4_____5  Comments:
Other:_____
1_____2_____3_____4_____5  Comments:


## *General Problem-Solving Skills*

Using a step-by-step problem-solving strategy
1_____2_____3_____4_____5  Comments:
Using appropriate conflict resolution strategies
1_____2_____3_____4_____5  Comments:
Dealing professionally with "difficult people"
1_____2_____3_____4_____5  Comments:
Thinking creatively about novel or new approaches to solving problems
1_____2_____3_____4_____5  Comments:
Handling issues of power and control professionally
1_____2_____3_____4_____5  Comments:
Other:_____
1_____2_____3_____4_____5  Comments:


## *General Interpersonal Skills*

Developing and maintaining positive relationships
1_____2_____3_____4_____5  Comments:
Demonstrating competence and confidence
1_____2_____3_____4_____5  Comments:
Projecting a positive and optimistic attitude
1_____2_____3_____4_____5  Comments:
Developing and maintaining trust with others
1_____2_____3_____4_____5  Comments:
Other:_____
1_____2_____3_____4_____5  Comments:


## *General Teaming Skills (METs, IEPTs, SSTs, Grade Level Meetings, Department Meetings, etc.)*

Being a positive and contributing team member
1_____2_____3_____4_____5  Comments:
Sharing control appropriately at team meetings
1_____2_____3_____4_____5  Comments:
Facilitating team meetings as appropriate
1_____2_____3_____4_____5  Comments:

Organizing and scheduling team meetings
1_____2_____3_____4_____5  Comments:
Other:_____
1_____2_____3_____4_____5  Comments:


## General Parent Collaboration Skills

Including parents in the decision-making process as appropriate
1_____2_____3_____4_____5  Comments:
Explaining information so that parents understand it
1_____2_____3_____4_____5  Comments:
Helping to problem-solve and develop intervention plans with parents
1_____2_____3_____4_____5  Comments:
Identifying resources for parents
1_____2_____3_____4_____5  Comments:
Other:_____
1_____2_____3_____4_____5  Comments:


## General Knowledge-Based Skills

Have adequate knowledge of curriculum areas
1_____2_____3_____4_____5  Comments:
Have adequate knowledge of behavioral intervention/classroom management strategies
1_____2_____3_____4_____5  Comments:
Have adequate knowledge of special education rules and regulations
1_____2_____3_____4_____5  Comments:
Other:_____
1_____2_____3_____4_____5  Comments:


*Additional Comments Concerning Collaborative Skills Strengths and Weaknesses:*

*II*

# RESEARCH AND MODELS FOR
# IMPROVING TEACHER QUALITY

# Longitudinal Study: Effects of Action Research on Educators' Professional Growth

*Sandy Alber, Sally Edgerton-Netke, and Bess Kypros*

*Action research is not new. In more than fifty years of dialogue about action research, one of the themes is action research as a vehicle for teacher growth. Most of the studies about how action research influences teachers' professional growth immediately follow the teacher's completion of the research project. In this study, the authors explored the long-term influence of action research. This study suggests that conducting action research has lasting influences on educational practices. Thus, the study supports the earlier assertions of the value of action research as an effective means to educational reform made by El-liott (1991), Hollingsworth and Sockett (1994), and Killion and Bellamy (2000). Not only do teachers continue to use their studies, they appear to have used them as stepping stones to continued growth. Because action research seems to have positive carryover in educators' professional lives, the authors conclude that action research courses have an important role in teacher education programs.*

## INTRODUCTION

$\mathcal{A}$ction research has been described as a tool for professional development for more than fifty years. It has been studied as a part of the school improvement and professional development school (PDS) movements. Teacher educators have studied how action research influences undergraduate and graduate students' learning. Professors have also studied their own practice by conducting action research studies. Because studies on the influence of action research on professional growth have been conducted shortly after educators have completed an action research cycle, there is a missing piece in the action research literature. That missing piece is the study of the long-term effects of action research on professional development. What then are the long-term effects of action research on professional development? This study was designed to answer this question.

## REVIEW OF RELATED LITERATURE

Action research is not new. Most authors attribute its origin to Corey (1953). Since that time, others have continued the discourse about action research. Altrich, Posch, and Somekh (1993) clearly described the action research cycle. Cochran-Smith and Llytle (1993), Livingston and Castle (1992), Mills (2003), Sagor (1992), and others provided texts on mentoring action research studies. Other scholars have studied the outcomes resulting from action research projects. In more than fifty years of dialogue about action research, several themes emerge. Many of the themes fall under the category of educational reform. Multiple authors assert that action research is a vehicle for educational change (Elliott, 1991; Hollingsworth and Sockett, 1994; Killion and Bellamy, 2000; Schön, 1983). These change processes and outcomes occurred along multiple paths.

One of the roads to change is professional development. The duration and intensity of professional development activities varies widely. It is widely believed that high quality professional development must be sustained, intensive, and data driven (Killion and Bellamy, 2000). Because action research incorporates the aforementioned practices, it is often discussed as a professional development activity (Alber, Kypros, and Edgerton, 2000; Borgia and Schuyler, 1996; Hillard, 1997; Miller and Pine, 1990). Specifically, action research is viewed as a way to provide sustained staff development (Alber, 1999; Sachs, 1999). One venue for high quality professional development is professional development schools (PDS) (Holmes Group, 1990).

As the PDS movement spread, action research studies became one of the methods for addressing educational reform in partnerships between institutions of higher education and pre-K through grade 12 schools. PDS partnerships address National Staff Development Council (NSDC) recommendations to create learning communities, provide leadership development, ensure equity, and include family involvement. Studies about action research in university–school collaboratives focus on efforts to tackle classroom and school, as well as how to alter teacher preparation programs (Abdal-Haqq, 1998; Alber, 1999; Galassi et al, 1999; Goswami and Stillman, 1987; Olson, 1988).

Action research is also being used a school improvement effort in schools that are not connected to universities as PDS partners. NDCS guidelines and state interpretations of these guidelines have influenced schools to use action research as staff development. The state of Maryland is a good example of this use of action research (Sachs, 1999). Bernauer (1999) describes how NSCD standards and action research resulted in school improvement in Pennsylvania, and Killion and Bellamy (2000) describe how data-driven decision making strengthened school improvement in Colorado.

Action research in higher education is not limited to work in PDS sites. It is conducted in undergraduate programs, especially in conjunction with student teaching experiences (Alber, Kypros, and Edgerton, 1997 and 1998; Carroll and Yarger-Kane, 2000; Kosnick, 2000). In graduate programs, action research often is a capstone experience in which students synthesize program content and apply lessons to improve teaching and learning in their own settings (Alber, Kypros, and Edgerton, 1997, 1998; Kirova-Petrova, Alber, and Briod, 2000; Stanford, 2001). Levin and Rock (2003) describe how collaborative action research promotes growth in both preservice and experienced classroom teachers. Finally, action research is used in higher education when faculty members study their teaching of action research courses (Adler, 2003).

Action research is identified as a vehicle for teacher growth. Many acknowledge Kemmis and McTaggert's (1988) contribution to the development of action research as a way for educators to study real problems. Action research is said to empower teachers (Bernauer, 1999; Kincheloe, 1991; Alber and Kypros, 1995; Alber, Kypros, and Edgerton, 2002). Action research promotes personal as well as professional growth (Alber, Kypros, and Edgerton, 2002). Most of the studies about how action research influences teachers' professional growth immediately follow the teacher's completion of the research project.

## THE STUDY

In this study, the authors explore the lasting influence of action research. They wondered what effects completing action research projects would have on educators two or more years after completion of their studies. The purpose of this study is to determine to what degree action research influenced practice over time and to learn in what way the action research influenced practice. The research team asked program graduates about the long-term effects of action research on their professional growth, professional practice, leadership, risk taking, empowerment, and advocacy. They also asked alumni to identify the extent they perceived barriers to implementing teacher research in their setting. Lastly, they asked what kind of barriers educators experienced when they continued to use their research projects in their professional lives.

*Participants*

Study participants were alumni of three graduate programs and one undergraduate program at three universities in the Midwest. The programs were conducted in suburban and urban settings. Two graduate groups worked in suburban settings, one graduate group worked in an urban area, and the undergraduate group worked in suburban and urban areas. Alumni graduated from one of the four programs between two and five years prior to the implementation of this study.

*Methods*

In order to understand how teachers perceive their action research projects influence their current practice, educators were asked to complete a survey. The survey was grounded in the research literature presented earlier in this paper. Content was reviewed by professors who have taught action research classes for more than ten years each. The survey was piloted with a group of students completing their action research projects. After multiple revisions of the survey, an eight-item questionnaire resulted.

The eight prompts were followed by a four point Likert-type scale [very likely (4), likely (3), somewhat likely (2), and not at all likely(1)] and a narrative probe about the rationale for the selected rank on the Likert scale. Respondents were asked to respond to all eight questions in terms of how their action research project influenced their current thinking and behaviors. Participants were asked to return their completed surveys in stamped envelopes included in the mailing. Upon return of the surveys, means for the numerical responses to Likert scale items were calculated and three readers examined the narrative responses for themes.

## FINDINGS

Seventy-two surveys were analyzed. Mean Likert scores were calculated and are reported by item as they appeared on the questionnaire. Presentation of identified themes for each narrative response follows the reporting of the means. Representative student comments are provided to clarify themes.

*Item 1: I continue to grow professionally.*

The mean score of 3.78 led the researchers to believe that alumni who did action research were very likely to continue to grow professionally. An analysis of the narrative comments resulted in two categories of professional growth. Forty-six percent of the comments related to others-led professional growth, and 45 percent of the comments related to self-directed professional growth. Alumni of graduate programs were twice as likely to engage in self-led professional development as undergraduate alumni. Examples of others-led professional development included participating in workshops or university programs. Examples of self-directed professional growth included "reading journals and articles" and "networking with other teachers."

Early childhood educators continued to grow professionally in a variety of ways, but most often they participated in short-term, informal education (workshops, conferences, etc.). Reading professional literature was the second most frequent way to grow professionally. Additionally, one graduate alumni group reported reading professional literature considerably more than other groups. Interacting with colleagues was the third most frequent path to professional growth. The fourth most frequent group of comments clustered around reflective practice. It is important to note that only graduate alumni reported engaging in reflective practice. Finally, 79 percent of the individuals list listed more than one way they continued to grow professionally.

*Item 2: I use my project when planning adult-child interactions.*

A mean of 3.5 indicated alumni were quite likely to use their research when planning and interacting with children. Graduate alumni perceived they continued to implement their projects more than undergraduate alumni. Students reported that they used their project when interacting with children in a variety of ways, but these ways tended to relate to curriculum and instruction. An alumnus wrote, "I keep in mind that all children are different and I have to develop a curriculum that will benefit them in my classroom." Undergraduate students more often reported projects to help them clarify their beliefs. An undergraduate alumnus wrote, "The data that I obtained and the reading I did for my project helped me define my beliefs; helped me strengthen the resolve I had about equity, gender, race, religion, etc."

Narrative comments were also analyzed to determine the extent to which alumni continued to use their projects. Most alumni, 48 percent, reported using their study frequently. An illustration of frequent use is "By exposing my students to more writing opportunities they have become wonderful writers." Another 24 percent reported that they used part of their projects. An alumnus wrote, "I still teach several of the units and activities that were thought up during my Master's Project." Finally, 9 percent said they elaborated on their original study. An example of elaboration was using a school-based study in the community. "I am the director of our VBS at South

Baptist Church—[I'm] using professional people to teach nutrition, crafts and exercise."

Some alumni reported that they used their study very little. Eighteen percent of the alumni reported that project use was not appropriate in their current position. An alumnus working in her home said, "I don't deal with children on a day-to-day basis, but the time I spent observing in the kindergarten room is very valuable to me."

*Item 3: I use my project when I plan adult-adult interactions.*

A mean of 3.14 indicated alumni were likely to use their study when working with families, colleagues, and community members. Both graduate and undergraduate alumni reported using their projects with adults, but undergraduate alumni were slightly less likely to do so. The analysis across programs showed that three of the programs from two universities were more likely to use their project work with families.

Fifty-four percent of the alumni used their projects with families. An example of using the project research with families from a graduate alumnus read, "I continue to use *all* effective means of communication with my parents and I encourage colleagues to do so as well. These are weekly newsletter, phone calls, communication folders and Family Funshops." An undergraduate response read, "I have developed and used activities (with parents) that promote cooperation, problem solving or using manipulative worksheets whenever possible."

Thirty-eight percent of the alumni reported using their projects with colleagues in workshops and by collaborating. "I have presented my unit at a kindergarten workshop district wide," wrote one former graduate student. Another former student wrote, "I discuss things learned with colleagues." Lastly, 8 percent of the alumni used their projects in the community. "Although I am not currently working, in social situations I present information concerning playground safety . . . I am often asked my opinion of different playground features" is one instance of using project work in the community.

*Item 4: I am a child and family advocate.*

The mean score of 2.96 showed that alumni were likely to use their research to be advocates. Three of the four groups said they were very likely to be advocates and a fourth group said they were somewhat likely to be advocates. The analysis of the narrative comments presented a different picture.

When sorting narrative comments, two groups, including the alumni who reported being somewhat likely to be advocates, reported considerably more examples of advocacy. Some of the examples reported as advocacy in two of the groups saying they were very likely to be advocates were not actually advocacy examples. An example of advocacy is "This year I have contracted three agencies outside of school to help with cases of abuse and need." A comment that appears not to be advocacy is "My room is always packed with choice." An example from alumni who said they were somewhat likely to be an advocate wrote, "[I] always feel guilty that I'm not doing more on the state level."

*Item 5: I assume leadership roles in my profession.*

A mean score of 2.45 showed that alumni perceived that they were somewhat likely to assume leadership roles. The analysis of narrative comments showed that there was a wide variety of ways educators were leaders. One group, a suburban graduate program, was more likely than the other groups to take multiple leadership roles. Leadership most frequently occurred in the professionals' work settings.

Sixty-eight percent of the examples related to work place settings, such as the following example. "I am a member of almost every committee in my building." Nineteen percent of the comments reflected leadership outside the work setting. An example of leadership in other settings is "I am currently the president of early childhood Lutheran educators in Southeast Michigan." Twelve percent of the comments indicated that alumni were not likely to be leaders at the time surveyed. For example, one alumnus wrote, "I am still new to the profession, so for now, I tread lightly." Another alumnus wrote, "I do not work outside of the home."

*Item 6: I take risks in my profession.*

The four groups responded differently to this prompt. The likelihood of taking risks varied by geographic location and tenure status. Undergraduates, nontenured educators, said they were not very likely (mean of 1.23) to take risks. Undergraduate comments aligned with their mean Likert scores because they most often reported that they did not take risks. One undergraduate alumnus wrote, "I do not have tenure yet!"

Urban teachers reported they were somewhat likely to take risks. Suburban teachers were very likely to take risks. The urban graduate alumni mean of 2.57 showed that they were somewhat likely to take risks. An example of urban risk taking is "I guess investing my 'life savings' in a business of authentic assessment is a risk!"

Suburban teachers were very likely to take risks. The two suburban graduate alumni groups very likely to take risks, as evidenced by means of 3.77 and

3.86. The narrative comments indicated the two suburban graduate groups were taking risks in the curriculum and instructional arena. An example of risk taking in the suburban groups is "I initiate programs. This takes dedication, persuasiveness, and creating change. This change often is risky personally for me as well as for others."

*Item 7: My project work empowered me.*

The mean of 3.88 showed that the groups believed that it was very likely that doing their action research projects empowered them. The analysis of narrative comments showed that three of the four groups felt empowered because they believed they were more knowledgeable. One of these three groups also indicated that they were empowered because doing their research projects gave them confidence. The fourth group believed they were more empowered because they were more likely to be advocates as a result of doing their project work.

Examples of graduate alumni empowerment follow. "The research made me a strong, more informed advocate for the rights of all children." "I feel so strongly about what I was taught, I applied for a position to share the experience." "I now feel like an expert when I speak to parents. I also feel like I am a better teacher." Examples from undergraduate alumni were similar to those of graduate alumni. "My work gave me information and knowledge to feel comfortable enough to share with parents." "I really grew as a professional and as a person."

*Item 8: There are barriers that keep me from implementing what I learned in my project.*

Respondents were not very likely to find barriers when attempting to use their studies. The mean score for this item was 1.27. Undergraduates were more likely to identify barriers. The barriers that they identified differed from barriers identified by graduate students.

Although respondents were not very likely to encounter barriers when attempting to use their research, the researchers were interested in finding out if there were clusters within the few barriers mentioned. The clusters of barriers were 1) uninformed colleagues and leaders (graduate alumni only), 2) lack of resources, 3) legislative and other mandates, and 4) newness to the job (undergraduate alumni only). Examples of these barriers follow. "The biggest barrier has been an uninformed group of colleagues and a principal who is learning, but still holds some strong beliefs himself." "Time constraints are a barrier." "My district mandates a set of assessments. We must use them with *no* alterations. Alternative assessments can be *very* useful."

Undergraduate alumni found the statement was somewhat true (mean of 2.11). The barriers reported were similar to those reported by graduate alumni. Unlike graduate alumni, undergraduate alumni did not find their colleagues a barrier. Outside influences was an undergraduate alumni barrier. One wrote, "The court system and stereotypes keep people from accepting fathers as valuable parents." Another barrier reported only by undergraduate alumni was lack of resources. An example follows: "The main barrier is no one has managed to find monies to buy transportation for HeadStart children and families." Finally, job status was the final barrier for undergraduate alumni. One reported, "I do not have my own classroom and can't set up a classroom the way I envision it."

## SUMMARY OF FINDINGS

All of the groups indicated that they were very likely to continue to grow professionally as a result of conducting action research. They were quite likely to use their research as they worked with children and were likely to use it when working with other adults. Three of the four groups said they were very likely to be a child advocate and the other group said they were somewhat likely to be advocates. All groups were likely or somewhat likely to assume leadership roles. Taking risk varied by years of experience and geographic location. All groups said it was very likely that their action research work had empowered them. Finally, the alumni found few barriers to implementing what they learned in their action research studies.

## DISCUSSION

This study suggests that conducting action research studies have lasting influences on educational practices. Thus, the study supports the earlier assertions of the value of action research as an effective means to educational reform made by Elliott (1991), Hollingsworth and Sockett (1994), Killion and Bellamy (2000), and Schön (1983). Not only do teachers continue to use their studies, but they also appear to have used them as stepping stones to continued growth. They read more, attend more workshops, assume leadership positions, take risks in their practice, and are likely to be child, family, and professional advocates. Graduate students who complete action research projects find few barriers to using or extending their research. Undergraduate students perceived more barriers.

Several trends were identified in the analysis of the narrative responses. All alumni groups believed they were more informed or expert in the field of early childhood education as a result of conduction their action research projects. They also had more confidence as a result of doing action research. Responses in this study confirm the idea that action research empowers educators (Bernauer, 1999; Kincheloe, 1991; Alber and Kypros, 1995; Alber, Kypros, and Edgerton, 2002). Interestingly, the analysis of narrative responses showed that all groups were likely to be child advocates, which contradicts the quantitative findings for the urban alumni. It is possible that the definition of advocacy is different for this group of educators. This advocacy item needs exploration.

Because action research conducted in graduate and undergraduate programs seems to have positive carryover in educators' professional lives, we conclude that action research courses have an important role in teacher education programs. In spite of the positive findings in this study, in order to make a stronger statement about the power of action research in teacher education programs, more research needs to be conducted. For example, alumni surveyed in this study were all from the same Midwestern state. It would be interesting to see how the survey results turn out in other settings. All of the alumni in this study were previously enrolled in early childhood education programs. It would be worthwhile to see if similar findings would occur in other education program and in professional development schools.

Seventy-two surveys is not a large number. The findings would be strengthened with a larger study. Because the data is self-reported data, it would be valuable to design a study to examine the long-term effects of action research using another method for data collection. Finally, timing of a study is an important consideration. Alumni in this study were surveyed just prior to the enactment of the No Child Left Behind legislation. It would be interesting to know if this legislation influenced responses to the questions in this study. Although this study confirms previous studies about the benefits of action research projects, the authors suggest additional research in understanding the long-term benefits of action research projects.

## REFERENCES

Abdal-Haqq, I. (1998). *Professional development schools: Weighing the evidence.* Thousand Oaks, CA: Corwin.

Adler, S. (2003). "Dilemmas of action research." *Action in Teacher Education, 25*(1), 76–82.

Alber, S. (1999). *How action research projects connect theory and practice in an urban professional development school.* Paper presented at the National Association for the Education of Young Children Conference. New Orleans, LA.

Alber, S., and Kypros, B. (1995). *Action research: Helping students develop and use their professional voices.* Paper presented at the National Association for the Education of Young Children Conference. Washington, DC.

Alber, S., Kypros, B., and Edgerton, S. (1997). *Action research: A constructivist approach to professional development.* Paper presented at the National Association for the Education of Young Children Conference. Los Angles, CA.

Alber, S., Kypros, B., and Edgerton, S. (1998). *Action research as professional development: A comparison of three programs.* Paper presented at the National Association for the Education of Young Children Conference. Toronto, ON, Canada.

Alber, S., Kypros, B., and Edgerton, S. (2000). *The action research cycle: Increasing the understanding of its theoretical framework, processes and procedures and research-based outcomes.* Paper presented at the National Association for the Education of Young Children Conference. Atlanta, GA.

Alber, S., Kypros, B., and Edgerton, S. (2002). *Listening to student voices: How action research projects influence early childhood professionals.* Paper presented at the Association of Teacher Educators Conference. Denver, CO.

Altrich, H., Posch, P., and Somekh, B. (1993). *Teachers investigate their work: An introduction to the methods of action research.* New York: Routledge.

Bernauer, J. (1999). "Emerging standards: Empowerment with purpose." *Kappa Delta Pi Record, 35*(2), 68–70.

Borgia, E., and Schuyler, D. (1996). "Action research in early childhood education." *ERIC Digest.* Urbana: University of Illinois.

Carroll, S., and Yarger-Kane, G. (2000). "Designing projects to promote student teacher inquiry: An evolutionary approach." *Action in Teacher Education, 22*(2), 90–99.

Cochran-Smith, M., and Llytle, S. (1993). *Inside/outside: Teacher research and knowledge.* New York: Teachers College Press.

Corey, S. (1953). *Action research to improve school practices.* New York: Columbia University Press.

Davis, B., Resta, V., Miller, K., and Fortman, K. (1999). "Beginning teachers improve classroom practice through collaborative inquiry." *Networks: An On-Line Journal for Teacher Research, 2*(2).

Elliott, J. (1991). *Action research for educational change.* Bristol, PA: Falmer.

Galassi, J., Brader-Araje, L., Brooks, L., Dennison, P., Jones, M., Mebane, D., Parrish, J., Richer, M., White, K., and Vesilind, E. (1999). "Emerging results from a middle school professional development school: The McDougle–University of North Carolina Collaborative Inquiry Partnership Group." *Peabody Journal of Education, 74*(3–4), 236–53.

Goswami, D., and Stillman, P. (Eds.). (1987). *Reclaiming the classroom: Teacher research as an agency for change.* Upper Montclair, NJ: Boynton/Cook.

Hillard, A. (1997). "The structure of valid staff development." *Journal of Staff Development, 18*(2), 23–33.

Hollingsworth, S., and Sockett, H. (Eds.). (1994). *Teacher research and educational reform: Ninety-third yearbook of the National Society for the Study of Education: Part I.* Chicago: University of Chicago Press.

Holmes Group. (1990). *Tomorrow's schools: Principles for the design of professional development schools.* Lansing, MI: Author.

Kemmis, S., and McTaggert, R. (1988). *The action research planner* (3rd ed.). Victoria, Australia: Deakin University Press.

Killion, J., and Bellamy, T. (2000). "ON the JOB." *Journal of Staff Development, 21*(1), 54–59.

Kincheloe, J. (2003). *Teachers as researchers: Qualitative inquiry as a path to empowerment.* London: Routledge/Falmer.

Kirova-Petrova, A., Alber, S., and Briod, M. (2000). "Action research as commencement." *Journal of Early Childhood Teacher Education, 21*(2), 235–48.

Kosnick, C. (2000). "Looking back: Six teachers reflect on the action research experience in their teacher education programs." *Action in Teacher Education, 22*(2), 133–42.

Levin, B., and Rock, T. (2003). "The effects of collaborative action research on preservice and experienced teacher partners in professional development schools." *Journal of Teacher Education, 54*(2), 135–49.

Livingston, C., and Castle, S. (1992). *Teachers and research in action.* West Haven, CT: NEA Library.

Miller, D., and Pine, G. (1990). "Advancing professional inquiry for educational improvement through action research." *Journal of Staff Development, 11*(3), 56–61.

Mills, G. (2003). *Action research: A guide for the teacher researcher* (2nd ed.). Upper Saddle River, NJ: Merrill.

Olson, L. (1988). "Children flourish here." *Education Week, 2*(18).

Sachs, A. (1999). "Solid foundation." *Journal of Staff Development, 20*(1), 23–24.

Sagor, R. (1992). *How to conduct collaborative action research.* Alexandria, VA: Association for Supervision and Curriculum Development.

Schön, D. (1983). *The reflective practitioner: How professionals think in action.* New York: Basic Books.

Stanford, R. (2001). "Five keys to unlock continuous school improvement." *Kappa Delta Pi Record, 38*(2), 89–92.

# Follow the Teacher Leaders: The Potential of Teacher Leadership to Close the Achievement Gap

*Pamela A. Morehead and Jumanne Sledge*

*Increasing student performance and raising academic achievement among students in urban, rural, and high poverty schools in general is fundamental to the success of American students. We posit that the work of the teacher leader is critical to the success of the school and holds potential to assist in closing the achievement gap in our urban, rural, and high poverty schools. Our assertion is one that begs a broader definition of teacher leader. Regardless of who is taking the lead, we remain hopeful that most teachers will follow as we look to a definition of teacher leadership that includes high expectations for all students, for without high expectations, even the best instructional methodology will not close the achievement chasm that exists in so many of our schools. This chapter explores the definition of teacher leadership to improve teacher quality in low performing schools.*

## INTRODUCTION

The pressure schools face in closing the achievement gap forces them to rely heavily on improving teacher quality and require guidance and support of teachers (Ball and Cohen, 1999). Changes in classroom practices that affect student achievement require extensive learning by teachers and present major challenges. The Teaching Commission (2004) released a report, *Teaching at Risk: A Call to Action*, which argues vehemently that "helping teachers to succeed and enabling our children to learn is an investment in human potential" (p. 11). The commission proposed setting high standards for teacher performance and student achievement through ongoing, focused professional development, yet schools and districts continue to deliver inadequate professional learning opportunities for teachers (Ball and Cohen, 1999; Laine and Otto, 2000).

The inadequate learning opportunities for teachers are even more detrimental in urban environments where 43 percent of urban teachers lack a major or minor in their teaching field, as compared to only 27 percent of teachers in more affluent schools (Ingersoll, 1999). Furthermore, the National Center for Education Statistics (2000) reported that 20 percent of teachers in urban schools have three or fewer years of teaching experience. "Low-income students and students of color continue to be taught disproportionately by the least experienced, least well-educated teachers and teachers who fail to meet their state's licensure and certification standards" (The Education Trust, 2003, p. 2). Students who depend on public schools the most consistently receive the least.

At the same time, urban, rural, and high poverty schools in particular continue to face a parallel challenge as recruitment and retention of highly skilled teachers is increasingly more difficult. Teachers in many of these schools work with student populations that are increasingly diverse. Many of these children are from low-income families and various cultural backgrounds including large populations of Latino/as and African-Americans. Low expectations or lack of knowledge of effective strategies for working with students in challenging contexts are ongoing concerns for teachers in schools with histories of poor school performance (Leithwood and Fullan, 2003).

## A GLANCE AT THE ACHIEVEMENT GAP

Increasing student engagement and raising academic achievement among students trapped in low performing school districts is fundamental to the success of American students satisfactorily accomplishing the rigors of the No Child Left Behind Act (2001). In fact, when legislators consider that the largest one hundred urban school districts serve nearly one-fourth (23 percent) of all public school students in this country and that these same students account for 30 percent of all American students living in poverty as well as 40 percent of all non-White students in the United States (Manpower Demonstration Research Corporation, 2003), it then becomes imperative that policy makers and educators work untiringly toward closing the achievement gap.

Despite the continued efforts to close the achievement gap, many urban youngsters consistently underachieve annually. Thus, the public view of urban education is one of schools failing to educate students, especially those characterized as minorities, including African-American, Latino/a, and Appalachian (Quiroz, 1997). When American school systems fail to educate their minority students, both economic and societal influences are negatively impacted. For example, among minority groups, African-American (Black) males are affected most adversely (Pinkney, 2000).

When Black male students are compared to other students by gender and by race, they consistently rank lowest in academic achievement (Ogbu, 2003). Additionally, Black male students have the worst attendance record and are suspended and expelled most often (Raffaele Mendez, 2003). Black males are most likely to drop out of school and most often fail to graduate from high school or to earn a General Educational Development (GED) test diploma (Pinkney, 2000; Roderick, 2003). Adult Black males lead the nation in being undereducated, unemployed, and incarcerated (Hornor, 2002; Pinkney, 2000).

Continued comparisons between White students and Black and Latino/a students highlight additional disparities. White students' achievement in reading, science, and math ranks second, fourth, and seventh when compared with students worldwide. Black and Latino/a students however rank twenty-sixth and twenty-seventh on the same basic skills (Bracey, 2002). If an American student is in the top economic quarter of the population, he or she has a 76 percent chance of getting through college and graduating by age twenty-four; conversely if the student is in the bottom quarter, he or she has a 4 percent chance of getting through college and graduating by age twenty-four (Loeb, 1999).

## A LIMITED DEFINITION OF TEACHER LEADER

Over the years, educators defined teacher leadership as support faculty such as social workers, department heads, master teachers, lead teachers, learning consultants, school improvement and curriculum chairs, and program coordinators. However, the realization of more traditional teacher leadership roles has not necessarily led to dynamic school reform. The literature is replete with both the formal and informal roles and work of teacher leaders. The more formal roles for teacher leaders are generally granted by school administration, and the work is often clearly defined for them. In many schools, the role of the teacher leader may be quasi-administrative (Smylie and Denny, 1990), which can lead to peer mistrust and ineffective support mechanisms.

Wasley (1991) found in multiple in-depth case studies that a significant tension existed between formal teacher leaders and their colleagues. He argued that teachers are more influential with their colleagues when they work collegially with their peers to evaluate instructional practices and the effects on student learning and achievement. Many educational researchers defined the informal yet powerful role and work of teacher leaders quite differently from the formal role.

The informal role of teacher leader is one that is "embedded in tasks and roles that do not create artificial, imposed, formal hierarchies and positions" (Darling-Hammond, Bullmaster, and Cobb, 1995, p. 89). Crowther, Kaagan,

Ferguson, and Hann (2002) identified the informal role as one that emerges based on qualities of great teaching behaviors. Teacher leaders possess exemplary behaviors such as dealing with challenges within the school, striving for pedagogical excellence, and working for positive changes in the best interest of the total school community (Neuman and Simmons, 2000; Spillane, Halverson, and Diamond, 2001). In a study by Snell and Swanson (2000), they found that certain teachers emerged as leaders based on their instructional expertise, collegial collaboration, and ability to be reflective practitioners. Ultimately, the teacher leaders felt compelled and confident to lead or were empowered by their peers.

Despite the increasing emphasis in the literature on more informal definitions of teacher leadership, the role and work of teacher leaders continue to reflect a more formal or traditional existence in practice (Archer, 2001; Guiney, 2001). Regardless of whether the role of the teacher leader is formal or informal, we posit that the *work* of the teacher leader is critical to the success of the school and holds potential to assist in closing the achievement gap.

We agree that teacher leaders must be highly qualified, that is, knowledgeable in content, in practice, about how children best learn, and in interpersonal skills. Our assertion is one that begs a broader definition of teacher leader. Regardless of who is taking the lead, we remain hopeful that most teachers will follow as we look to a definition of teacher leadership that includes high expectations for all students. Without high expectations, even the best instructional methodology will not close the achievement chasm that exists in so many of our schools.

## AN EXPANDED DEFINITION OF TEACHER LEADER

Many educators and policy makers have the idea that teachers who are held to high performance standards in their content areas and possess a myriad of instructional strategies are effective teachers or "highly qualified." This idea has become the solution for closing the achievement gap. For teachers, are being "smart enough" and "resourceful enough" the only essential addends that result in increased student achievement? Acknowledging this phenomenon, what then prevents teachers from locating and teaching to student strengths? Legislators and many external influences believe that the answer to this question is teacher quality. In 2000, states received federal dollars, Title II grants, to improve teacher quality through use of content-specific professional development. Thus, the common definition of teacher quality espoused by legislators is one that identifies teacher quality as content-based knowledge.

While content knowledge comprises a portion of teacher quality, another much less supported component of teacher quality is often left unaddressed—teacher expectations. Ronald Ferguson (2003) presented evidence that suggested teachers' perceptions, expectations, and behaviors probably does help sustain, and perhaps even expand, the test score gap between White and African-American students. A teacher's beliefs ultimately influence teaching practices and behaviors (Good and Brophy, 1997). Delpit (1995) described the problem succinctly, "We say that we believe all children can learn, but few of us really believe it" (p. 172).

When educators have low expectations of student learning, the outcomes are the implementation of less challenging curriculum and ineffective instruction despite exposure to varied techniques or best practices. In order to make use of subject matter knowledge and differentiated instructional modes, the teacher has to fundamentally *believe* that the use of these techniques will make a difference in the students and their academic performance. Further, this fundamental belief, or lack thereof, influences the teaching habits and practices.

All too often disadvantaged children are subjected to school influences that erode their self-confidence, whereby teachers expect low performance and the children "live down" to these expectations in a self-fulfilling prophecy (Green, 1996). Delpit (1995) lamented, "It is hard to believe that these children can possibly be successful after their teachers have . . . so much negative indoctrination . . . there is a tendency to assume deficits in students rather than to locate and teach to strengths" (p. 172).

Over the past forty years, there have been several studies that support the claim that when teachers expect more, teachers get more. In Green's work (1996), he reviewed and analyzed the following studies: McDill et al. (1976); Beez (1968); Tuckman and Bierman (1971); Dusek (1975); Brohpy and Everston (1976); Brookover and Lezotte (1977); Crano and Mellon (1976); Smead (1981); and Rutter (1982). From his analyses, Green concluded American scholars have well documented and supported the finding that low expectations result in low student performance. Nonetheless, our attempts to close the achievement gap continuously ignore teacher expectations. More recently, Stone and Lane (2000) found that teacher expectations for student performance were a critical factor that explained a significant amount of variability in performance among Maryland students on state standardized exams using growth models.

The wisdom of expanding the definition of teacher quality to include teacher expectations is quite simplistic. If teachers expect success from all students, then it is not possible to leave a child behind. Teachers deliver instruction more effectively and enthusiastically for students for whom they have high expectations. Additionally, teachers respond more favorably to students for whom they have high expectations. As a result, student efficacy and academic performance are increased (Comer, 1996; Monroe, 1999).

## OPPORTUNITIES FOR TEACHER LEADERS

The dissonance between what we say and actually do in classrooms presents a great opportunity for teacher leaders; those who possess the essential keen substantive content knowledge, pedagogical knowledge, and interpersonal skills to support other teachers and ultimately close the achievement gap. Changing low expectations presents a daunting and impracticable challenge for teacher leaders. In fact, "leadership lies in the capacity to deliver disturbing news and raise difficult questions in a way that moves people to take up the message without killing the messenger" (Heifetz and Linsky, 2002, p. 74).

As teacher leaders utilize their interpersonal abilities to build trusting, communicative, and collaborative relationships with teachers over time, change will occur. Teacher leaders must champion the need for high expectations. This work includes eliminating the walls of personal and professional bias, ethnicity, socioeconomic status, culture, and gender. According to Green (2003), when the professional staff begins with sincerity to believe that all students can achieve, hold high expectations for student accomplishments, and do whatever it takes to ensure that students will learn, then the school operates in a climate of effectiveness that translates into gap closing efforts.

Attitudes and beliefs that teachers hold are highly personal and are therefore difficult to change. Attempting to positively affect the attitudes and beliefs of other teachers is a major responsibility for teacher leaders and may be the most complex task to undertake. Teacher leaders must look to the experts as they embrace the challenge and opportunity to support teachers in the change process. Hilliard (1991) proposed that deep restructuring and fundamental change occurs when we allow teachers to experience the joy of collaborative discussion, dialogue, critique, and action research.

While these critical conversations must begin, conversations alone are not enough to get all teachers to become reflective practitioners. Teachers must examine their beliefs about their expectations of students. Teacher leaders must begin to nudge teachers to shift their thinking and practices. Substantive reflection provides a process of pedagogical analysis leading to positive change.

## SPECIFIC SUGGESTIONS FOR EDUCATORS

A powerful and potentially underused professional development exercise is reflection. Maintaining high expectations for students' and teachers' beliefs in self-efficacy are common among teachers who are reflective practitioners (Collinson, Killeavy, and Stephenson, 1999; Cruickshank and Haefele, 2001). Teacher leaders can support colleagues by examining the realities of their classroom (e.g. achievement data, class diversity profile) and assist them in reflecting on their practices. In doing so, teacher leaders can use the Socratic method—posing questions about instructional practices, assessment, and student/teacher relationships to help classroom teachers begin to make necessary changes to best meet the needs of their students.

Support of teachers to the aim of meeting the needs of their students occurs in many forms—modeling best practices, book clubs/professional reading, peer observations, ongoing assessment and evaluation, and grade level collaborative meetings to name a few. Teacher leaders must agree to support the teachers as they attempt to try new techniques and make use of the new information they acquire. In this type of culture, a professional learning community forms, and teacher leaders can continually focus the school community on Dufour and Eaker's (1998) three key reflective questions:

1. What do we want students to know and understand?
2. How will we know when they know it?
3. What will we do when they don't?

These basic yet "getting to the heart of the matter" questions center teachers on their pedagogical practices. By posing these questions, the reflection that occurs focuses teachers on the importance of having intimate knowledge of the curriculum, ongoing assessment, and research-based instructional practices. Tantamount to curriculum, assessment, and instruction is an understanding of how children best learn. Our deep understanding of how children best learn requires us to know and reach the whole child (e.g. academically, culturally, personally). We maintain that the complexity of this depth of understanding commands leadership beyond the role of the principal alone.

According to Crowther et al. (2002), "Teacher leadership facilitates principled action to achieve whole-school success. It applies the distinctive power of teaching to shape meaning for children, youth, and adults. And it contributes to long-term, enhanced quality of community life" (p. 10). As teacher leaders build capacity for professional learning communities, shared leadership increases. Equally as important, the opportunity for teacher leaders to support colleagues in an analysis and challenge of their beliefs about student learning also occurs. Improving teacher quality is critical within low-income and urban schools. As teachers follow their own leaders, the resulting community of learners holds great promise for low-performing schools to improve professional practice and ultimately close the achievement gap.

## CONCLUSION

In a knowledge-saturated, informational, and technological age, we argue that for students to excel teachers themselves need to possess requisite knowledge in their content areas. We further posit that the requisite knowledge should be accompanied or sanctioned by the teacher's state licensure or credentialing guidelines. Regrettably, what is least understood and often ignored is the teacher's need to set and maintain high expectations for his or her students.

If we aim to close the achievement gap between minority and nonminority students, between high-income and low-income students, between suburban and urban students, and between English-speaking students and limited English proficient students, then we must address what teachers understand and believe about these distinct populations. Principals cannot shoulder this responsibility alone. The potential of teacher leadership to lead others along a path of improvement must be considered by schools in desperate need of improvement. As good leaders, we must invite teachers to follow us in reflecting upon the expectations they hold for *all* students. Then and only then, we will begin to better define teacher quality and look toward closing the achievement gap.

## REFERENCES

Archer, J. (2001). "Profession: Teach, or consequences." *Teacher Magazine, 2*(7), 6–8.

Ball, D. L., and Cohen, D. K. (1999). "Developing practice, developing practitioners: Toward a practice-based theory of professional education." In L. Darling-Hammond and G. Sykes (Eds.), *Teaching as the learning profession* (pp. 3–31). San Francisco: Josey-Bass.

Beez, W. V. (1968). "Influence on biased psychological reports of teacher behavior and pupil performance." *Proceedings of the 76th annual convention of the American Psychological Association, 3,* 605–606.

Bracey, G. W. (2002). *Put to the test: An educator's and consumer's guide to standardized tests.* Bloomington, IN: Phi Delta Kappan International.

Brophy, J., and Everston, C. (1976). *Learning from teaching: A developmental perspective.* Boston: Allyn and Bacon.

Brookover, W., and Lezotte, L. (1977). "*Changes in school characteristics coincident with changes in student achievement.*" East Lansing: Michigan State University College of Urban Development.

Carano, W. D., and Mellon, P. M. (1978). "Casual influence of teachers expectancies on children's academic performance: A cross-lagged panel analysis." *Journal of Educational Psychology, 70*(1), 39–49.

Collinson, V., Killeavy, M., and Stephenson, H. J. (1999). "Exemplary teachers: Practicing an ethic of care in England, Ireland, and the United States." *Journal for a Just and Caring Education, 5*(4), 349–66.

Comer, J. (1996). *Rallying the whole village: The Comer process for reforming education.* New York: Teachers College Press.

Cruickshank, D. R., and Haefele, D. (2001). "Good teachers, plural." *Educational Leadership, 58*(5), 26–30.

Crowther, F., Kaagan, S. S., Ferguson, M., and Hann, L. (2002). *Developing teacher leaders: How teacher leadership enhances school success.* Thousand Oaks, CA: Corwin Press.

Darling-Hammond, L., Bullmaster, M. L., and Cobb, V. L. (1995). "Rethinking teacher-leadership through professional development schools." *The Elementary School Journal, 96*(1), 87–106.

Delpit, L. (1995). *Other people's children: Cultural conflict in the classroom.* New York,: The New Press.

Dufour, R., and Eaker, R. (1998). *Professional learning communities at work: Best practices for enhancing student achievement.* Bloomington, IN: National Educational Service.

Dusek, J. B. (1975). "Do teachers bias children's learning?" *Review of Educational Research, 4* (45), p. 661–84.

The Education Trust. (2003). *In need of improvement: Ten ways the U.S. Department of Education has failed to live up to its teacher quality commitments.* Washington, DC: Author.

Ferguson, R. F. (2003). "Teachers' perceptions and expectations and the black-white test score gap." *Urban Education, 38*(4), 460–507.

Good, T. L., and Brophy, J. E. (1997). *Looking in classrooms* (7th ed). New York: Longman.

Green, R. L. (1996). "A profile of African American males." In B. W. Austin (Ed.), *Repairing the breach.* Dillon, CO: Alpine Guild.

Green, R. L. (2003). *Evaluation of school improvement in the Detroit Public Schools—phase 2 final report.* East Lansing: Urban Affairs Program, Michigan State University.

Guiney, E. (2001). "Coaching isn't just for athletes." *Phi Delta Kappan, 82*(10), 740–43.

Heifetz, R., and Linsky, M. (2002). "A survival guide for leaders." *Harvard Business Review, 80*(6), 65–74.

Hilliard, A. (1991). "Do we have the will to educate all children?" *Educational Leadership, 49*(1), 31–36.

Hornor, L. L. (Ed.). (2002). *Black Americans: A statistical sourcebook.* Palo Alto, CA: Information Publications.

Ingersoll, R. (1999). "The problem of under qualified teachers in American secondary schools." *Educational Researcher, 28*(2), 26–37.

Laine, S. W. M., and Otto, C. (2000). *Professional development in education and the private sector: Following the leaders.* Oak Brook, IL: North Central Regional Educational Laboratory.

Leithwood, K., and Fullan, M. (2003). "What should be the boundaries of the schools we need?" *Education Canada, 43*(1), 12–15.

Loeb, P. R. (1999). *Soul of a citizen: Living with conviction in a cynical time.* New York: St. Martin's Press.

Manpower Demonstration Research Corporation. (2003). "Big city school districts face a big job." *Fast Fact Archive.* Retrieved from www.mdrc.org.

McDill, E. L., Meyers, E. D., and Rigsby, L. C. (1967). "Institutional effects on the academic behaviors of high school students." *Sociology of Education,* 2(40), p. 181–89.

Monroe, L. (1999). *Nothing's impossible: Leadership lessons from inside and outside the classroom.* New York: Public Affairs.

National Center for Education Statistics. (2000). *Education Statistics Quarterly,* 2(4): Author.

Neuman, M., and Simmons, W. (2000). "Leadership for student learning." *Phi Delta Kappan 82*(1), 9–12.

Ogbu, J. U. (2003). *Black American students in an affluent suburb: A study of academic disengagement.* Mahwah, NJ: Lawrence Erlbaum Associates.

Pinkney, A. (2000). *Black Americans* (5th ed.). Upper Saddle River, NJ: Prentice Hall.

Quiroz, P. A. (1997). *The "silencing" of the lambs: How Latino/a students lose their voice in school.* East Lansing: Julian Samora Research Institution, Michigan State University.

Raffaele Mendez, L. M. (2003). "Who gets suspended and why: A demographic analsis of school and disciplinary infractions in a large school district." *Education Treatment of Children, 26,* 30–51.

Roderick, M. (2003). "What's happening to the boys? Early high school experiences and school outcomes among African American male adolescents in Chicago." *Urban Education, 38,* 538–607.

Rutter, M., Manghan, B., Mortimer, P., Ouston, A., and Smith, A. (1979). *Fifteen thousand hours: Secondary schools and their effects on children.* Cambridge: Harvard University Press.

Smead, V. S., and Chase, C. I. (1981). "Student expectations as they relate to achievement in 8th grade mathematics." *Journal of Educational Research* 6, 115–20.

Smylie, M. A., and Denny, J. W. (1990). "Teacher leadership: Tensions and ambiguities in organizational perspective." *Educational Administration Quarterly, 28*(2), 150–84.

Snell, J., and Swanson, J. (2000). *The essential knowledge and skills of teacher leadership: A search for conceptual framework.* Paper presented at American Education Research Association. New Orleans, LA.

Spillane, J. P., Halverson, R., and Diamond, J. B. (2001). "Investigating school leadership practice: A distributed perspective." *Educational Researcher, 30*(3), 23–28.

Stone, C., and Lane, S. (2000). *Relationship between changes in MSPAP school performance over time and teacher, student, and school factors.* Paper presented at National Council on Measurement in Education. New Orleans, LA.

The Teaching Commission (2004). *Teaching at risk: A call to action.* New York: The Teaching Commission, CUNY Graduate Center.

Tuckerman, B., and Bierman, M. (1983). "Beyond pygmalion: Galetea in the schools." Paper presented at the annual meeting of the American Educational Research Association.

U.S. Congress. (2001). *No Child Left Behind Act of 2001.* Public Law 107-110. 107th Congress. Washington, DC: Government Printing Office.

Wasley, P. D. (1991). *Teachers as leaders: The rhetoric of reform and the realities of practice.* New York: Teachers College Press.

# · 7 ·

# Infusing Technology to Increase Teachers' Comfort Level and Likelihood of Use

*Anne Tapp, Poonam Kumar, and Elizabeth A. Hansen*

*The purpose of this study was to examine the impact of integrating technology in a science methods course on preservice teacher comfort level with computer technology. One hundred and ten preservice teachers were administered a pre- and post-test measuring their level of familiarity and comfort with each skill as well as their likelihood of use within a classroom. Technology was infused within a university science methods course. Preservice teachers were given instruction on each technology skill in context as well as opportunities to practice teaching each within a classroom setting. Results indicated that preservice teachers' comfort level significantly increased as did their likelihood of teaching this skill within the classroom.*

## INTRODUCTION

In recent years there has been an increased emphasis both at the national and state levels for training teachers to integrate technology in their classrooms. The International Society for Technology in Education (ISTE) has developed guidelines and standards for technology competencies for teachers. Many states have adopted the ISTE standards for teacher preparation and require teachers to be competent in the use of technology.

Schools have significantly increased the availability of computers and technology in recent years. It is estimated that about 98 percent of the public schools in the United States now have access to the Internet (U.S. Department of Education, 2001). However, despite the increased access to technology in schools, very few teachers use computers for instruction and most do not use technology to promote critical thinking and problem-solving skills in students (Hunt and Bohlin, 1995; Office of Technology Assessment, 1995; Yildirim, 2000).

A national survey conducted by the Education Market Research for *Education Week*'s 1999 National Survey of Teachers' Use of Digital Content reported that "Nearly four out of ten teachers say their students don't use classroom computers at all during a typical week," and 35 percent of the teachers reported they did not have enough training to use the technology (Albee, 2003; Moursund and Bielefeldt, 1999). Similarly, the Office of Technology Assessment (1995), in a survey of graduates, found that while more than half reported being prepared to use simple computer applications like drill and practice, tutorials, games, word processing, and publishing applications, only less than 10 percent felt competent to use sophisticated applications like multimedia and presentation packages, electronic network collaboration capabilities, or problem-solving applications.

The National Center for Education Statistics (NCES, 2000) also reported that 70 percent of the teachers felt that they were not prepared to use computers and the Internet in their instruction. These reports also suggest that very few teachers are using technology for instructional purposes.

Research indicates that lack of adequate training and experience is one of the main reasons teachers do not use technology in their teaching (Thorsen and Barr, 1997; Vagle and College, 1995; Yaghi, 1997; Yildirim and Kiraz, 1999; Yildirim, 2000). Most of the university teacher training programs in the United States require preservice teachers to take one computer literacy course. This course usually focuses on basic computer applications and software, such as word processing, spreadsheets, e-mail, and Internet. The computer literacy course may be enough to teach students some basic computer applications, but this isolated computer course is not enough to prepare teachers to use technology in their instruction.

Due to the lack of adequate training and experience with using technology in an instructional context, teachers do not know how to infuse technology in their own teaching, and they do not feel very comfortable using it (Abbott and Faris, 2000; Albee, 2003; Ropp; 1999; Thorsen and Barr, 1997). Technology should be infused in methods courses to provide preservice teachers more experiences in using technology in instructional contexts. In this chapter, the authors discuss how they infused technology in a science methods course for elementary preservice teachers and the impact of technology integration on preservice teachers' comfort level with technology and their likelihood of use.

## METHODS

It was hypothesized that if teachers are given lessons on how to integrate technology and an opportunity to practice these skills by implementing lessons within their field, their comfort level with technology and their likelihood of use would also increase. One hundred and ten preservice teachers enrolled in a Midwestern university science methods course within a two-year period of time were included in the study. The science methods course contained a field component to allow students the opportunity to put their knowledge and skills into practice. Within the semester timeframe, teams of three students were assigned to urban and rural elementary classrooms for seven three-hour blocks.

A pre-test and post-test were designed by the course instructor using the course objectives and ISTE standards for the purpose of assessing students'

**Table 7.1.   Pre-test and Post-test Questionnaire**

How familiar (F) and comfortable (C) are you with the following? (*1 not at all to 4 very familiar or comfortable*)
Place an X in the box to show your likelihood of using this concept or skill within the classroom at this time. (*1 not likely to 4 very likely*)

|  | *1* | *2* | *3* | *4* |
|---|---|---|---|---|
| Example |  | X | F | C |
| MI curricular frameworks |  |  |  |  |
| Science benchmarks |  |  |  |  |
| GLASS |  |  |  |  |
| MI CLIMB |  |  |  |  |
| MI BIG |  |  |  |  |
| National Science Education Standards |  |  |  |  |
| Project 2061/AAAS |  |  |  |  |
| Virtual field trips |  |  |  |  |
| WebQuests |  |  |  |  |
| Science assessment |  |  |  |  |
| Internet as an instructional tool |  |  |  |  |
|  | *1* | *2* | *3* | *4* |
| Science MEAP goals and objectives |  |  |  |  |
| Inquiry |  |  |  |  |
| Constructivism |  |  |  |  |
| Blackboard® discussion forum posting |  |  |  |  |
| Blackboard® group functions |  |  |  |  |
| Blackboard® live chat |  |  |  |  |
| Evaluating websites for classroom use |  |  |  |  |
| Internet Searches (like Google or Yahoo) |  |  |  |  |
| Distance learning |  |  |  |  |
| Online collaboration |  |  |  |  |
| Electronic portfolios |  |  |  |  |

prior knowledge about science pedagogy, methodology, technology, and progress. Another goal was to evaluate the instructor's effectiveness in meeting course objectives. The pre-test was administered to the preservice teachers at the beginning of the first science method class meeting (see table 7.1). Students rated their level of familiarity and comfort with various areas within science education as well as computer technology skills. They also included their likelihood of using each within a classroom setting.

The undergraduate teacher education program in this Midwestern university has a required technology course that focuses on technology skills. Sixty-four percent of the students self-reported concurrent enrollment in this course while 10 percent had reported successful completion of this course. Within the science methods course, the preservice teachers received instruction on the integration of various computer technology skills into practice while receiving instruction on science methodology and pedagogy.

The technology component to the lesson was solely to be used to enhance the lesson. The idea that technology is not used for technology's sake but used to enhance curriculum was discussed and modeled. Metacognition, thinking about one's own thinking and learning, was also used to identify each skill in context. The preservice teachers integrated these computer technology skills within their lesson planning and implemented them within the field component of the methods course.

The focused technology skills taught within the context of elementary science education included virtual field trips, distance learning, evaluation of websites, online collaboration, WebQuest construction, and electronic portfolios. Collaborative teams of three students were required to develop elementary science lessons including these technology skills and deliver them in their field placement. Students individually presented their lessons.

Examples of these technology enhancements to the lessons include

- a fifth grade class taking a virtual field trip inside the human respiratory system following their dissection of pigs' lungs;
- groups of third graders at three different elementary schools posting online weather data to compare and contrast and then asking questions of a Weather Channel meteorologist via distance learning; and
- second graders working their way through the solar system within a WebQuest.

All lessons met content standards and benchmarks and used technology to enhance the subject matter.

The classroom teacher and university instructor or field supervisor were present to offer instant feedback and an opportunity to immediately debrief with each student. Following the three-hour block, all students debriefed as a

**Table 7.2.  Weighted Averages of Data**

| | Familiarity Pre | Familiarity Post | Comfort level Pre | Comfort level Post | Use Pre | Use Post |
|---|---|---|---|---|---|---|
| Virtual Field | 1.32 | 3.95 | 1.06 | 3.84 | 1.09 | 3.88 |
| WebQuest | 1.15 | 3.93 | 1.05 | 3.87 | 1.05 | 3.91 |
| Internet Tool | 2.24 | 3.99 | 1.50 | 3.97 | 1.31 | 3.99 |
| Eval Web | 1.85 | 4.00 | 1.48 | 4.00 | 1.35 | 3.99 |
| Searches | 3.47 | 3.99 | 3.31 | 3.97 | 3.15 | 3.98 |
| Dist.Learn | 1.38 | 3.99 | 1.11 | 3.96 | 1.01 | 3.95 |
| Online Colla | 1.04 | 3.92 | 1.00 | 3.87 | 1.00 | 3.82 |
| Eportfolio | 1.08 | 3.85 | 1.00 | 3.76 | 1.00 | 3.80 |

whole group with their university instructor and field supervisors. This gave students the ability to learn from their peers' strengths and weaknesses as well as offer suggestions, ideas, and support.

These opportunities were also made available to students within their Blackboard® online community. Blackboard® is a web-based course-building/ e-learning program that enables instructors to present course content to their students on the web. Students had the ability to participate within an open class discussion forum as well as a group forum created for just their collaborative, three-person teams. Within the group forums, students had their own discussion board, e-mail and file exchange function, and virtual chat area. Students utilized both the whole class and small-group forums.

At the last class meeting, the preservice students were administered a post-test containing the same items as the pre-test (see table 7.2). They again rated their familiarity and comfort levels with various areas within science education and computer technology skills and identified their likelihood of using each within a classroom setting. The students provided narrative comments on their progress, comfort, likelihood of use, and benefit to the host institution.

## DISCUSSION

The analysis (see appendix A at end of chapter) supported the hypothesis that as comfort level with technology concepts and skills increases, the likelihood of using these technology concepts and skills within the classroom increases. The analysis shows that there is a strong relationship between familiarity and comfort level in using technology concepts and skills. In this particular design, it was not possible to separate the effects of familiarity and the effects of comfort level in the result of the increase in the use of technology. Clearly, both of these factors are related to the use of technology concepts and skills in the classroom.

The strongest correlation was between pre-assessment comfort level and pre-assessment use. This indicates that comfort level with technology could have been the most important factor before the training/learning intervention. It could be said that the training/learning intervention was so successful that the student's familiarity and comfort level with the technology concepts and skills were elevated so high as to increase the likelihood of the students' incorporating the technology into their classroom.

The student comments (see appendix B at end of chapter) support the analysis of the survey data. This study indicates that the infusion of technology into the science methods courses along with instruction on how to integrate technology into teaching science coupled with an opportunity to practice the technology skills is a powerful learning intervention. Teaching technology skills is not enough. The integration of technology needs to be modeled by the methods instructor, and the preservice teachers need an opportunity to practice the skills.

## CONCLUSION

The reviewed literature suggests teachers are not prepared to properly utilize computer technology within their classrooms and very few are using technology for instructional purposes. Research findings indicate that preservice teachers need more than the basic required educational technology course, which offers these skills in isolation, to possess a likelihood of utilizing computer technology within their classroom. Having the opportunity to practice these skills in context within their field experiences increases their comfort level and likelihood of use.

The instructional delivery within this study included university classroom instruction of computer technology within the context of science education. Also included was student planning of lessons incorporating computer technology as an enhancement to the lesson and the teaching of these lessons to their assigned classroom of students. Students were placed in collaborative teams of three, though they each took turns with lesson delivery. Instructors, field supervisors, and peers were present to give instant feedback and support. The use of Blackboard® afforded students another opportunity to collaborate and offer support at the whole class and collaborate group levels.

Teacher education institutions need to take a critical look at their programs to evaluate true effectiveness. To strengthen the likelihood of classroom utilization of computer technology, preservice teachers need to practice these skills within the context of a classroom setting. Teaching these computer technology skills in isolation has been proven ineffective at meeting the needs of our nation's teachers. The demonstrated effectiveness of the stated model within this study could serve as an effective example. It would be recommended that preservice teachers have additional opportunities to practice these skills within all methods courses including reading, social studies, and math to further strengthen their level of comfort and likelihood of use within these curricular areas.

One of the comments from a participant sums up how technology training in the science methods classroom can make a difference. This student speaks to the comfort level and how his/her confidence was increased: "I'm really glad we got to practice this now before getting our own classrooms. I didn't know if I could do it, and now I do."

## REFERENCES

Abbott, J. A., and Faris, S. E. (2000). "Integrating technology into preservice literacy instruction: A survey of elementary education students' attitudes toward computers." *Journal of Research on Computing in Education, 33*(2), 149–61.

Albee, J. (2003). "A study of preservice elementary teachers' technology skill preparedness and examples of how it can be increased." *Journal of Technology and Teacher Education, 11*(1), 53–71.

Hunt, N. P., and Bohlin, R. M. (1995). "Events and practices that promote positive attitudes and emotions in computing courses." *Journal of Computing in Teacher Education, 11*(3), 21–23.

Moursund, D., and Bielefeldt, T. (1999). *Will new teachers be prepared to teach in a digital age? A national survey on information technology in teacher education.* Santa Monica, CA: Miliken Exchange on Education Technology. (ERIC ED 428 072).

National Center for Education Statistics. (2000). *Public school teachers' use of computers and the Internet.* Washington, DC: U.S. Department of Education.

Office of Technology Assessment, U.S. Congress. (1995). *Teachers and technology: Making the connection.* OTA-EHR-616. Washington, DC: U.S. Government Printing Office.

Ropp, M. M. (1999). "Exploring individual characteristics associated with learning to use computers in preservice teacher preparation." *Journal of Research on Computing in Education, 31*(4), 402–23.

Thorsen, C. D., and Barr, R. D. (1997). "Computer competencies for teacher educators." In J. D. Price, K. Rosa, S. McNeil, and J. Willis (Eds.), *Technology and teacher education annual* [CD-ROM]. Charlottesville, VA: Association for the Advancement of Computing in Education.

U.S. Department of Education, National Center for Education Statistics. (May 2001). *Internet access in U.S. public schools and classrooms: 1994–2000.* Washington, DC: U.S. Government Printing Office.

Vagle, R., and College, D. (1995). "Technology instruction for preservice teachers: An examination of exemplary programs." In D. Willis, B. Robin, and J. Willis (Eds.), *Technology and teacher education annual—1995* (pp. 230–37). Charlottesville, VA: Association for the Advancement of Computing in Education.

Yaghi, H. M. (1997). "Pre-university students' attitudes toward computers: An international perspective." *Journal of Educational Computing Research, 16,* 237–49.

Yildirim, S. (2000). "Effects of an educational computing course on preservice and inservice teachers: A discussion and analysis of attitudes and use." *Journal of Research on Computing in Education, 32*(4), 479–96.

Yildirim, S., and Kiraz, E. (1999). "Obstacles to integrating online communication tools into preservice teacher education: A case study." *Journal of Computing in Teacher Education* 15(3), 23–28.

## APPENDIX A

The data was drawn from the pre-assessment of 110 students and the post-assessment of the same students. The students ranked their responses to familiarity from 1 = not at all to 4 = very familiar. The students ranked their comfortableness from 1 = not at all to 4 = very comfortable. The students also ranked their likelihood of using the concepts or skills within the classroom from 1 = not likely to 4 = very likely. The concepts/skills were Virtual Field Trips, WebQuests, Internet as an Instructional Tool, Evaluating Websites for Classroom Use, Internet Searches (like Google or Yahoo), Distance Learning, Online Collaboration, and Electronic Portfolios.

Weighted averages were calculated for the student's responses for the pre-assessment and the post-assessment of familiarity with the concepts/skills, comfort level with the concepts/skills, and likelihood of use of the concepts/skills. Table 7.2 shows the data for each of the categories.

A correlation was done between the six weighted totals: Pre-Assessment Familiarity, Post-Assessment Familiarity, Pre-Assessment Comfort Level, Post-Assessment Comfort Level, Pre-Assessment Use, and Post-Assessment Use. There was a strong correlation of .963 between the Pre-Assessment Familiar-

**Table 7.3.    Correlation between Six Weighted Totals and Data Analysis**

|  | Pre Familiar | Post Familiar | Pre Comfort | Post Comfort | Pre Use | Post Use |
|---|---|---|---|---|---|---|
|  | Column 1 | Column 2 | Column 3 | Column 4 | Column 5 | Column 6 |
| Column 1 | 1.00 |  |  |  |  |  |
| Column 2 | 0.61 | 1.00 |  |  |  |  |
| Column 3 | 0.96 | 0.47 | 1.00 |  |  |  |
| Column 4 | 0.63 | 0.94 | 0.50 | 1.00 |  |  |
| Column 5 | 0.94 | 0.41 | 1.00 | 0.44 | 1.00 |  |
| Column 6 | 0.69 | 0.92 | 0.54 | 0.92 | 0.48 | 1.00 |

ity and the Pre-Assessment Comfort Level. There was a strong correlation of .938 between Pre-Assessment Familiarity and Pre-Assessment Use. The regression analysis showed significance at the .01 level ($p = .00058$). There was a strong correlation of .942 between Post-Assessment Familiarity and Post-Assessment Comfort Level. There was a strong correlation of .924 between Post-Assessment Familiarity and Post-Assessment Use. The regression analysis showed significance at the .01 level ($p = .001029$). There was a strong correlation of .996 between Pre-Assessment Comfort Level and Pre-Assessment Use. The regression analysis showed significance at the .01 level ($p = 1.91E-0$). There was a strong correlation of .922 between Post-Assessment Comfort Level and Post-Assessment Use. The regression analysis showed significance at the .01 level ($p = .001114$). Table 7.3 shows the correlation data for each of the categories.

## APPENDIX B: STUDENTS' NARRATIVE COMMENTS DEMONSTRATING PROGRESS, COMFORT, LIKELIHOOD OF USE, AND BENEFIT TO HOST INSTITUTION

In addition to responding to the pre-test and post-test questionnaires, preservice teachers showed gains in likelihood of use within a classroom when sharing comments.

The following comments demonstrate an increase in computer skills:

- The word computer used to make my skin crawl. Not anymore. I didn't know how totally cool it could be when planning and doing lessons. Our kids loved my project!
- I was doubtful that I would be able to do these things. They aren't too hard, and I now know they are well worth any effort put in. I'm working on another webquest now.
- No one in my family can believe I created the things I did and taught the things I did during my science lesson in field. (including me) They are proud, and I'm proud of myself.

These comments show an increase in likelihood of computer technology use:

- How did I teach before without technology? I can't wait to be able to use them again in field and when student teaching. I don't want to be without it ever again!

- I love using computers for teaching.
- I can't wait to use these things with my own class.
- I never realized how many computer applications there were in the elementary classroom. I can't wait to use all of them in my classroom some day.
- Webquests are a great tool. There are so many things you can do with them, and students are motivated to complete them.
- I didn't know how many great things there are to do in a classroom with technology. Wow! I can't wait to use them again. The students and we had so much fun, and they learned so much.
- I wish they had the internet when we were in elementary school. There is so much you can do with it. I can't wait to see what will be available for students and teachers twenty years from now.
- Technology in the classroom is really great. Our students said they liked our virtual field trip better than the ones they had physically been on this year.
- Thanks for helping us get NASA scheduled for our distance learning. The kids couldn't believe we were live with Houston. I bet they will always remember this one. I will.
- It was cool to compare and contrast data with other students around the country. The students thought so too. I can't believe how much they learned on so many levels. All classrooms need to use the internet for quality lessons. The possibilities are endless.
- I'm really glad we got to practice this now before getting our own classrooms. I didn't know if I could do it, and now I do. Our students and I loved these lessons! I can't wait to use these things with my own students someday soon. (I hope.)
- Computer technology needs to be present in each classroom. Why isn't it? Teachers who don't use it are holding their students back. There are so many things you can do with technology that you can't touch without it.
- I can't believe there are people who know about technology in the classroom and don't use it. They must be able to see the value, don't they? Why wouldn't they want their students to have the best experiences they can?
- I'm now disappointed my children's school doesn't do much with computer technology. I never knew its value until I used it myself with our science field students. I hope I can make a difference and let people know how very important this is. I want my kids to have these amazing opportunities.

The following comments show a benefit to the school partner:

- We were able to teach our teacher how to evaluate web sites. She said she was going to take the information to her next staff meeting. She was surprised and glad.
- We were able to show our field teacher how useful technology can be. We left our tools and projects for her to use and showed her a few things. Our students heard us talk and they were really glad.

# Preservice Teachers' Knowledge Development in Reading Instruction

## Guidi Yang

*This study explored twenty-two preservice teachers' knowledge development in reading instruction through self-examination of their own beliefs about reading and teaching reading in the elementary classroom over an initial reading methods course. Findings show that the course had an impact on shaping the preservice teachers' beliefs and knowledge development in reading instruction.*

## INTRODUCTION

Beliefs play a central role in learning experience and achievements (Cotterall, 1999). Educational research shows that there is a correlation between teachers' beliefs and their instructional practices. For example, Alexander and Dochy (1995) report that beliefs play a distinctive role in "the way teachers define the learning environment or respond to particular instructional materials or approaches" (p. 144).

Although some studies examined preservice teachers' beliefs and their belief change over the course of preservice teacher education methods classes, few addressed preservice teachers' beliefs about reading and their theoretical orientations to reading instruction. Moreover, no study to date in the field of reading instruction investigated both preservice teachers' beliefs about reading and theoretical orientations to reading instruction at the same time. Given this gap, the current study was conducted to shed some insights on the topic for teacher educators in reading education when helping preservice teachers develop their knowledge about reading and reading instruction.

# LITERATURE REVIEW

In her discussion about learner beliefs, Wenden (1986) considers it necessary to discover students' beliefs or knowledge about their learning and to provide activities that would allow students to examine their beliefs and the possible impact on how they approach learning.

Based on their review of research on student cognition and conceptual change, Pintrich, Marx, and Boyle (1993) summarize that "students' prior conceptual knowledge influences all aspects of students' processing of information from their perception of the cues in the environment, to their selective attention to these cues, to their encoding and levels of processing of the information, to their search for retrieval of information and comprehension, to their thinking and problems solving"(p. 167). They further point out that students' conceptual change is influenced by personal, motivational, social, and historical factors.

Over the years, the impact of courses on student beliefs has also been investigated. Wallhausen (1990) conducted a study to examine the effect of a course in teaching reading and language arts on preservice teacher education students' perceptions and found that students master the basic content of reading theory and methodology more rapidly than they change their beliefs about reading theory and instructional methodology; students' abilities to change their beliefs about the reading process and to accommodate new models are tied to their level of cognitive development and their motivation to mediate change; students who are motivated to change their beliefs are more apt to mediate change when they have the opportunity to observe more than one active model of instruction; and students not adequately prepared to implement an unfamiliar reading strategy in a teaching situation will resist implementing new strategies and fall back on old models.

After a two-year study on preservice teachers' theoretical orientations to the reading process and the relationship between undergraduate coursework and student teaching experiences to the orientations, Wham (1993) reports that half the students experienced no changes in theoretical orientations. Those who changed coursework had greater influence than student teaching. In a longitudinal study that examines beliefs and perceptions of elementary and secondary preservice teachers concerning the concept of integrated teaching, Reinke and Moseley (2002) found that the coursework portion of the program provided statistically significant positive changes about the integration of subjects in the classroom. Similar results were generated from other subject areas in teacher education, such as math (Hart, 2002) and physical education (Sofo and Curtner-Smith, 2004).

Studies were also conducted to investigate how to design instructional activities in teacher education programs to assist preservice teachers in identifying their beliefs (Asselin, 2000). In this regard, Freese's study (1999) on the role of reflection on preservice teachers' knowledge development shows that reflection is an effective tool in teacher preparation. Therefore, he advocates that preservice teachers should be encouraged to develop, identify, and reflect upon their own beliefs about teaching and learning.

## DEFINITIONS OF TERMS

The following are some reading-related terms and definitions used in this study.

*Top-down view:* According to *A Dictionary of Reading and Related Terms* (Harris and Hodges, 1981), it is "a theoretical view of reading as a process of using one's experiences and expectations in order to react to text and build comprehension. In top-down processing, comprehension is seen as reader-driven, rather than text-driven" (p. 332).

*Bottom-up view:* According to Harris and Hodges (1981), it is "a theoretical position that comprehension in reading consists of the accurate, sequential processing of text. In bottom-up processing, comprehension is seen as text-driven: it is built up and governed by the text only, and does not involve the reader's inner experiences and expectations" (p. 38).

*Interactive view:* According to Harris and Hodges (1981), it is "a theoretical position that reading involves both the processing of text and the use of experiences and expectancies the reader brings to the text, both sources of information interacting and modifying each other in reading comprehension. In interactive processing, comprehension is generated by the reader under the stimulus control of the print" (p. 160).

*Phonics:* According to Harris and Hodges (1981), it is "an approach to the teaching of reading and spelling that stresses symbol-sound relationships, especially in beginning reading instruction" (p. 238).

*Skills:* According to Vacca, Vacca, Gove, Burkey, Lenhart, and McKeon (2003), it is "based on the assumption that learning to read successfully presumes the acquisition of a finite but sizable number of skills and specific abilities" (p. 614).

*Whole language*: According to Vacca et al. (2003), it is "a theoretical perspective that focuses on the integration of all the language arts—reading, writing, speaking, and listening—to create child-responsive environments for learning that are supported by literature-based instruction" (p. 615).

## METHODS

This study was designed to investigate how some preservice teachers developed their knowledge about reading instruction through self-examination and identification of their own beliefs about reading and their theoretical orientations to teaching reading in the elementary classroom over an initial reading methods course. Specifically, the study focused on two research questions: 1) What are the preservice teachers' beliefs about reading and their theoretical orientations to reading instruction? 2) Will there be changes in preservice teachers' beliefs about reading and their theoretical orientations to reading instruction after taking a one-semester reading methods course? In addition, the study examined how the preservice teachers viewed their knowledge development and interpreted their changed or stable beliefs and theoretical orientations over the course of the methods class. Finally, the impact of the course on the preservice teachers' knowledge development in reading instruction was explored.

The participants were a group of twenty-two preservice elementary teachers who were taking an initial reading methods course, Teaching Reading in the Elementary Classroom, at a university in the United States. The preservice teachers were requested to respond, both at the beginning and conclusion of the methods course, to ten 'beliefs about reading' interview questions under the subtitle, *What Do You Believe about Reading and Learning to Read?* in their textbook *Reading and Learning to Read* (Vacca et al., 2003).

Then they analyzed and compared their beliefs with the sample responses provided in the appendix of the textbook. Based on the comparison, they determined whether they viewed reading and learning to read from one of the three views of reading: top-down, bottom-up, or interactive. The preservice teachers were also requested to examine which of the three theoretical orientations, namely phonics, skills, and whole language, they held using the DeFord Theoretical Orientation to Reading Profile (DeFord, 1985) each time they responded to the 'beliefs about reading' interview questions.

Based on the results generated from identifying their beliefs and theoretical orientations, both at the beginning and conclusion of the course, the preservice teachers used reflective journals to discuss what their beliefs and theoretical orientations were and whether their beliefs about reading and reading instruction had changed over the reading methods course. They were also invited to provide a rationale for the "change" or "unchange" of their beliefs and theoretical orientations. The reflective journals were not graded so that preservice teachers felt free to express their beliefs, thoughts, and feelings.

Data collected from the reflective journals were analyzed by calculating percentages and qualitatively according to the three views of reading—bottom–up, top-down, and interactive—and three theoretical orientations—phonics, skills, and whole language. In the process, attention was also directed to the question whether the preservice teachers had changed their beliefs and theoretical orientations, as well as the relationship between their knowledge development and the reading methods course.

## RESULTS

Overall, data showed that the majority (72.73 percent) of the preservice teachers viewed reading and learning to read from an interactive perspective, which is highly advocated in the field of reading instruction. Three held the top-down view (13.64 percent), and another three (13.64 percent) had the bottom-up perspective. As for the theoretical orientations, 50 percent preservice teachers found that their perspectives fell into the category of phonics. Twenty-seven percent were for skills, and 13.64 percent were for whole language. However, 4.55 percent had the orientation between skills and phonics, and another 4.55 percent claimed to have the theoretical orientation between phonics and whole language. In terms of changes in beliefs about reading and theoretical orientations to reading instruction as a result of the reading methods course, twelve (54.54 percent) reported that their beliefs had not changed, while ten (45.45 percent) stated that they had changed their beliefs.

Following is a more detailed qualitative presentation of the data collected from the preservice students' reflective journals, based on the categories indicated in the reading interview and the Theoretical Orientation to Reading Profile.

### The Top-Down View

As mentioned earlier, only 13.64 percent of the preservice teachers held a top-down view of reading. One of the students wrote, "I marked most top-down responses." She supported her beliefs by stating that the goal of reading instruction was to "increase comprehension." And she continued,

> If either a first- or sixth-grade reader pronounced a word wrong, or substituted another word, but the replacement word still made sense in the passage, I would not correct the word.

Even though they preferred the top-down view, they did not limit themselves to it. For example, a student stated that she also felt "young children need to be drilled on phonics."

### The Bottom-Up View

The percentage of preservice teachers who held a bottom-up view coincided with that of the top-down view believers. One student stated, "I strongly believe in the bottom-up approach. I believe it is important for students to make letter-sound associations, build sight vocabulary, sound out words, and learn the meanings of those words." Another student expressed a similar view:

> I am a firm believer in the bottom-up model. It is a type of reading model that assumes that the process of translating print to meaning begins with the printed word and is initiated by decoding graphic symbols into sound.

Still another wrote the following based on her general understanding,

> Just like anything in life, whether it is reading or being on a new job, you have to start from the bottom and work your way up. From the first day of class up until now I have believed in the bottom-up theory and all it has to offer.

Like those who believed in the top-down view, bottom-up believers did not limit themselves to one reading view. Here are two examples. One student stated,

> I like the idea of teaching phonics and the bottom-up approaches. Although I strongly believe in the bottom-up model and phonics, I don't necessarily push aside what other models and theoretical orientations have to say.

Another wrote,

> I believe mainly in the bottom-up approach. But there are a few instances where I would like to use the top-down model. So in the real world classroom, I would use a combination of the two methods.

*The Interactive View*

About 73 percent of the preservice teachers believed in the interactive view of reading. They not only identified their views about reading and reading instruction, but they also gave reasons why they held an interactive view. One student wrote,

> I concluded that I hold largely an interactive belief system that integrates both bottom-up and top-down beliefs. Being familiar with both belief systems allows me to implement a wide range of strategies best suited to the individual students.

A second student stated,

> My beliefs about teaching reading in the classroom are interactive. While vocabulary is an important part of activities that involve reading, comprehension is the main goal of reading in the end.

A third had these lines,

> I have found that I like the interactive belief system the best because it involves recognizing and using background information to uncover or make predictions about the unknown.

A fourth put, "I found that I was a firm believer in the interactive approach because I felt strongly toward both the bottom-up and top-down approaches." To support her statement, she related her own classroom teaching experience:

> When I did reading groups with a second grade classroom and a student made an error, I would not interrupt if it still made sense. If the error changed the meaning of the sentence, then I would intervene and correct the mistake. When the students approached a word that they did not know, however, I would help them sound out the word, give them phonetic clues, and help them come to a result. Overall, I incorporated both approaches in my teaching practice.

While expressing their own beliefs about reading, the preservice teachers also indicated that they would strive for a balance in reading instruction. Here are two examples.

> I think that the only way to maintain balanced instruction is to incorporate all beliefs and present all methods and techniques, and all views toward reading.

My answers were divided evenly between bottom-up and top-down. Therefore, my beliefs align with the interactive model. I believe that parts of each model are useful. In order to do the best, the models should be combined.

*Phonics*

Fifty percent of the preservice teachers claimed that their theoretical orientation was phonics. Here are two of the statements from their reflective journals.

> The results showed that I believe in the phonics approach, which I deem accurate as it is important to teach the relationships between letters and sounds.

> I firmly believe that phonics and phonemic awareness play the number one role in learning to read. Students lacking the ability to sound out words and differentiate between different consonants and the sounds they make when put together are clearly headed for trouble.

Some preservice teachers were aware of a broad range of perspectives in reading instruction, indicating that they would apply other approaches when needed or as necessary. Here is a statement, "My theoretical orientation continues to be based on phonics, but not limited to phonics." Another student had the similar view:

> Phonics, I believe, is a great place to start in reading instruction, but it is not complete because phonics readers do not resemble most trade books or reading materials that students will encounter. Students should be taught phonics strategies as a method of word attack so that when they are faced with an unknown word, they don't get discouraged and stop reading.

*Skills*

Twenty-seven percent of the preservice teachers chose skills perspective as their theoretical orientation. However, some identified themselves as believers of both phonics and skills or phonics and whole language orientations. Following are some of the statements.

> My score for the test makes me a skills believer and I agree with that observation.

My score lies on the border between phonics and skills orientations. Skills are needed for cognitive and language development and I plan to use both theories in my classroom.

### Whole Language

About 14 percent of the preservice teachers chose whole language as their theoretical orientation. One stated, "For the *DeFord Theoretical Orientation to Reading Profile*, I found out that I am a believer in the whole language curriculum." Some gave interpretations for their orientation. For example,

> Whole language means focusing on the integration of all the language arts—reading, writing, speaking, and listening to create a child responsive environment for learning.

> Whole language offers repetitions and practice which are imperative to become a fluent reader and writer.

While claiming whole language as their theoretical orientation, some also realized that they should not limit themselves to one theoretical orientation.

> Whole language is a good model and should be looked at as a goal for reading instruction. But again, it is not complete because it does not provide any "hints" like word attack strategies to help students in comprehension.

Interestingly, even those who did not take whole language as their theoretical orientation mentioned the term in their journals, expressing an understanding of the importance to incorporate different theories in reading instruction. Here is what one student wrote,

> Although whole language was not my theoretical orientation, I believe it is important to incorporate all theories in lesson plans to suit the needs of all children and to provide variety and spice to the classroom.

### Changes of Beliefs

Changes of beliefs and theoretical orientations over the course of the semester were observed by both the preservice teachers themselves and the instructor. Statistically, 45 percent thought they had changed their beliefs and theoretical orientations. Here are some of the statements.

At the beginning of the semester I thought I was a top-down believer, but over the course of this semester my beliefs have changed.

I was very surprised at my final results in that I am a believer in the top-down approach. I have been a phonics guy for most of my life. I guess that I must have realized that comprehension is what reading is really about.

The first time I took the "Profile," I was considered to have a phonics theoretical orientation. After taking this course and learning more concrete ideas and theories about teaching reading in the elementary classroom, the score I received after taking the test for a second time put me in the skills-based orientation. I am not surprised at this change.

## No Change of Beliefs

Findings also revealed that 55 percent of the preservice teachers did not change their beliefs and theoretical orientations about reading and reading instruction. Here is a representative statement.

The views that are reflected in the scores of these interviews and surveys are quite similar to the views that I had at the beginning.

While stating that there was no change in their views and theoretical orientations, some preservice teachers also reflected on the reasons for their findings. For example, one student tried to connect her present beliefs with her future classroom practice, predicting a belief change in a real world classroom.

Although I have gained substantial knowledge about the process of learning to read and learned many different professional views on the best method, I did not really expect to change my views based on classroom learning. I predict that my views on the best methods will remain unchanged until I have experienced significant work in my own classroom.

## Early Years of Literacy Experience Mattered

Findings also indicated that the preservice teachers' beliefs about reading were highly correlated with the way they learned to read in their early literacy development years. This is the case with phonics believers in particular. For instance, those who identified phonics as their theoretical orientation were the ones who stated that they had been taught to learn to read through phonics instruction and regarded themselves as good readers. Following are two cases in point.

My personal views have not changed. When I was young, phonics was the method that made me an effective reader. I feel that phonics has had the greatest impact upon my learning to read.

I was a firm believer in phonics. This was most likely because as a child learning to read, I was taught with phonics. That was the method that all of my teachers used.

## The Impact of the Course

Data from the preservice teachers' reflections also showed that the course had a positive impact on the preservice teachers' knowledge development. In addition, it had helped them shape and reinforce their beliefs about reading and their theoretical orientations to reading instruction. Following are some of the comments from the students' reflective journals.

I have learned many things in the class and everything has shaped my beliefs.

I believe many of my beliefs and ideas about reading have changed throughout the semester because I have acquired new information about reading.

Having no real change in my views on reading and reading instruction does not mean that I have not learned anything this semester. Through class discussions, readings, and observations in the real world classroom, the beliefs that I had about reading and reading instruction have been positively reinforced. Everything that I have experienced throughout this semester has helped me define exactly what my beliefs are called.

This course has given me more insight into teaching literacy to elementary age children. I have developed as a person and feel more confident in the classroom and with my preferred style of teaching.

I believe that my score has changed from the beginning of the semester to now because I have learned a lot of new materials about reading in the classroom and my outlook on reading is different from what it was before.

One student even thought that the course had helped her develop her own reading strategies and desire to read. She wrote,

Before this class I didn't have the desire to read. I would only ever read if it was an assignment. Even in high school I only read if I had to. During this class, I have developed a greater desire to read. I started to realize that I am never going to be able to teach reading if I don't like to read. I need to have a desire to read in order to instill a desire in my students.

### *The Preservice Teachers' Related Thoughts*

While identifying and reflecting on their beliefs and theoretical orientations, the preservice teachers shared other related thoughts on reading instruction, ranging from their past learning experience to their own role as a teacher in the future classroom. Some even shared their willingness to change their beliefs once they are in a real world classroom. Here is one comment.

It will be very interesting to see if my beliefs alter at all once I become a certified teacher and if so, what they will change to.

Some preservice teachers commented that identifying and reflecting on their beliefs and theoretical orientations regarding reading and reading instruction were useful in the process of their knowledge development. Some students wrote the following:

Completing the interview and profile was an effective way of summing up the beliefs and values that I have constructed and reflected upon throughout the semester.

I think that reflecting on how our views and beliefs have changed throughout the course of the semester is a positive way to show our growth. I have opened my eyes to many new ideas and that can only be a good thing.

Though I had my beliefs, I had no idea how to categorize or characterize my thoughts on the topic of reading and reading instruction. Now, with a well-defined framework on my viewpoint on reading and reading instruction, I was able to further understand lessons, practices, and methods that reinforced my ideas.

This interview provided me with a clear vision of why exactly I believe in the bottom-up model.

## CONCLUSION

This study investigated some preservice teachers' knowledge development in reading instruction through self-examination of their own beliefs about reading and theoretical orientations to teaching reading in the elementary classroom over an initial reading methods course. Data analysis of the preservice teachers' reflective journals not only identified their beliefs and theoretical orientations but also showed that certain beliefs and theoretical orientations the majority of the preservice teachers held are encouraging as they are the views and orientations highly advocated by professionals in the reading field.

In addition, findings indicated that the course had a positive impact on the preservice teachers' knowledge development and helped them shape and reinforce their beliefs about reading theories and reading instruction. Finally, it is worthwhile to point out that the process of guiding the preservice teachers to identify and reflect on their views, beliefs, and theoretical orientations to reading instruction itself proved to be a good instructional tool to promote and assess student knowledge development in teacher education courses.

## REFERENCES

Alexander, P. A., and Dochy, F. J. (1995). "Conceptions of knowledge and beliefs: A comparison across varying cultural and educational communities." *American Educational Research Journal, 32*(2), 413–42.

Asselin, M. (2000). "Confronting assumptions: Preservice teachers' beliefs about reading and literature." *Reading Psychology, 21*(1), 31–55.

Cotterall, S. (1999). "Key variables in language learning: What do learners believe about them?" *System, 27,* 493–513.

DeFord, D. E. (1985). "Validating the construct of theoretical orientation in reading instruction." *Reading Research Quarterly, 20,* 366–67.

Freese, A. R. (1999). "The role of reflection on preservice teachers' development in the context of professional development school." *Teaching and Teacher Education, 15*(8), 895–909.

Harris, T. L., and Hodges, R. E. (1981). *A dictionary of reading and related terms.* Newark, DE: International Reading Association.

Hart, L. C. (2002). "Preservice teachers' beliefs and practice after participating in an integrated content/methods course." *School Science and Mathematics, 102*(1), 4–14.

Pintrich, P. R., Marx, R. W., and Boyle, R.A. (1993). "Beyond cold conceptual change: The role of motivational beliefs and classroom contextual factors in the process of conceptual change." *Review of Educational Research, 63*(2), 167–99.

Reinke, K., and Moseley, C. (2002). "The effects of teacher education on elementary and secondary preservice teachers' beliefs about integration: A longitudinal study." *Action in Teacher Education, 24*(1), 31–39.

Sofo, S., and Curtner-Smith, M. D. (2004). "Influence of a critically oriented methods course and early field experience on preservice teachers' conceptions of teaching." *Sport, Education and Society, 9*(1), 115–42.

Vacca, J. A., Vacca, R. T., Gove, M. K., Burkey, L., Lenhart, L. A., and McKeon, C. (2003). *Reading and learning to read* (5th ed.). New York: Allyn & Bacon.

Wallhausen, H. A. (1990). "The effect of first teacher education courses on students' perception of the reading process." (ERIC ED 322490).

Wenden, A. (1986). "What do second-language learners know about their language learning? A second look at retrospective accounts." *Applied Linguistics,* 7(2), 186–205.

Wham, M. A. (1993). "The relationship between undergraduate course work and beliefs about reading instruction." *Journal of Research and Development in Education,* 27(1), 9–19.

# Measuring the Gap between Knowledge and Teaching: The Development of the Mathematics Teaching Profile (MTP)

*Naomi Jeffery Petersen*

*Teacher quality is a focus of concern in the No Child Left Behind Act of 2001, high-lighting the need for valid instruments to assess pedagogical skill. Presented here is the Mathematics Teaching Profile (MTP), designed in collaboration between the School of Ed-ucation and the Department of Mathematics at Indiana University South Bend. Follow-ing a review of the theoretical and empirical basis for defining quality instruction using best practices, the technicalities of developing the instrument are discussed as well as the choices of statistical processes to reduce the data to meaningful constructs. Practical uses of the in-strument will be discussed, that is, as a formative assessment tool for professional develop-ment, and an evaluation tool for programs implementing reform-based innovations.*

## INTRODUCTION

$\mathcal{A}$s part of its strategy for every student to demonstrate adequate yearly progress, the No Child Left Behind Act of 2001 also sets a goal of every class-room staffed with a highly qualified teacher. This provided the impetus and the funding (through the Indiana Commission for Higher Education) for an am-bitious professional development effort by teacher educators at Indiana Uni-versity South Bend. The Mathematical Proficiency through Inquiry-Based Teaching and Learning project was implemented for two years (2003–2004 and 2004–2005) with fifth through eighth grade mathematics teachers from schools in the South Bend/Elkhart, Indiana, area. This project addressed the need for this population of teachers to deepen and broaden their mathemati-cal knowledge and their repertoire of effective mathematics teaching strategies and to improve the mathematical performance of students, for "Although teachers may understand the mathematics they teach in only a superficial way, simply taking more of the standard college mathematics courses does not appear to help matters" (Kilpatrick et al., 2001, p. 373).

In each year of the project, teachers participated in a two-week workshop during the summer and followed up with online discussions, work, and classroom visits and videotaping during the school year. The project directors, Anne Brown and Paulette Zizzo, from the Department of Mathematical Sciences at Indiana University South Bend, led the summer workshops and school-year activities. Sara Sage, from the School of Education at IUSB, conducted the overall external project evaluation, including qualitative methods; Naomi Jeffery Petersen, also from the School of Education, assisted with the modification and development of instruments used as pre- and post-tests (Sage and Petersen, 2005). One instrument is introduced here: the Mathematics Teaching Profile (MTP) (Petersen, Sage, Brown, and Zizzo, 2003).

Of the nine goals of the project, three specifically address the gap between knowledge and teaching and are the focus of the instruments to be described:

1. Teachers will deepen and broaden their knowledge of the mathematics they teach;
2. Teachers will gain knowledge of various aspects of inquiry-based teaching and learning; and
3. Teachers will gain knowledge of the model for mathematical proficiency and how it relates to academic standards.

There is a profound difference between understanding mathematical concepts and procedures and using that knowledge to design effective instruction for a real group of students. Teaching any content area requires decisions that consider the content and the students as well as the professional knowledge base of what tends to be effective in helping the students achieve the content. Therefore, it is useful to discuss mathematical content, mathematical learning, and mathematics teaching before introducing the instruments used to measure changes in the gap.

## DEFINING MATHEMATICAL CONTENT

The National Council of Teachers of Mathematics (1989) was the first of the many discipline-based organizations to publish standards defining its content, articulating a paradigm shift from teaching mathematics as skill-oriented to a more conceptual understanding of deep subject-matter knowledge (AAAS, 1989). This was influenced in part by meaningful learning theory (Ausubel,

1968), structuralist epistemology (Gardner, 1972), and the related spiral curriculum model (Bruner, 1950).

Its importance in the field was spurred by the Nation at Risk (1983) report, manufactured or not (Shulman, 1987). Following the bipartisan approval of NCLB (2001), nearly all states adopted carefully articulated standards of content to be learned, or as the state of Washington terms them, Essential Academic Learning Requirements. In all cases, the standards emphasized "higher levels of thinking" beyond simple calculations, and high-stakes tests are used to measure their mastery.

The context of this discussion is the dilemma of implementing reform-era standards: the challenge to mathematics educators was to figure out what standards-based instruction really meant. The 1989 standards triggered a backlash of concern that procedural skills were neglected in favor of abstract concepts (Jackson, 1997). The "back to basics" essentialism, which fuels the current accountability reforms, tends to focus on the procedural skills while the education profession continues to develop a more sophisticated framework that requires more sophisticated teaching. This is complicated by the gap between the common understanding of adequate mathematical knowledge and that of the professionals.

This is true in other disciplines as well. For instance, although "good writing is good thinking," the Michigan Educational Assessment Program (MEAP) emphasizes formulaic composition, which drives teachers of English to forego the rich opportunities to develop meaningful ideas and more effective expression (Winerip, 2005).

The debate continues, for example, in the phonics wars, with the false dichotomy between process and product, with classroom teachers taking a utilitarian approach of accommodating that which is mandated, utilizing that which is familiar and intuitively effective, and avoiding distractions from the work at hand. Professional development must therefore address all three areas of professional knowledge: subject area content, student development, and teaching methods. As von Glasersfeld (1997) pointed out:

> Those who have picked up something useful, have memorized algorithms and routines, and even so, the "knowledge" they have acquired varies to an astonishing degree. None of this seriously impedes their ability to pass tests, because most tests require no more than repeating what was heard or read during the course. (p. 209)

The variance of teachers' knowledge base is indeed great and the very focus of the demand for higher quality teachers. However, American teachers have less time and resources for professional development than most developed countries (Ma, 1999), perpetuating the myth that teachers have static attributes.

As listed above, the first three goals of the workshop were to deepen teachers' subject matter and pedagogical knowledge in order to design instruction that develops deep mathematical knowledge in the students. This raises the issue of how learning occurs, best understood before presuming to teach.

## DEFINING THE LEARNING PROCESS

Long gone is the notion that children are tabula rasa, or blank slates on which to write whatever lessons are imposed by the teacher. Just as conceptions of mathematics have been articulated and corresponding misconceptions the focus of remediation, conceptions of learning have also been more specifically described. Unlike mathematics, however, there have been some major shifts in conceptions of learning, which in turn have influenced conceptions of the teaching of mathematics and all subjects.

As mentioned by the National Research Council in its synthesis of educational psychology, "views of how effective learning proceeds have shifted from the benefits of diligent drill and practice to focus on students' understanding and application of knowledge" (Bransford, Brown, and Cocking, 1999, p. xii). This is clearly aligned with the notion that subject area knowledge includes deep understanding, echoing the content debate of process versus product. Ideological differences are central to the discussion, in its practical application to teaching, for assumptions of learning guide the choice of instruction.

## DEFINING QUALITY MATHEMATICS TEACHING

The definition of quality teaching is left to the states, although the means by which they define quality are not. Empirical research is required, which in turn requires valid instruments in order to measure the constructs of interest. This requires a clear definition of the constructs to be measured, which is problematic because there is a great difference between traditional teaching methods and those found to be most effective.

### Do We Know What Practices Are Best?

Empirical and theoretical support for recognizing "best practice" was carefully synthesized by editors Kilpatrick, Swafford, and Findell (2001) in *Adding It Up*. Based on the overwhelming empirical support for using inquiry methods, chapter 10 presented the five-strand "teaching for mathematics proficiency" model that Brown and Zizzo adopted to design the professional development workshop:

1. *conceptual understanding* of the core knowledge required in the practice of teaching;
2. *fluency* in carrying out basic instructional routines;
3. *strategic competence* in planning effective instruction and solving problems that arise during instruction;
4. *adaptive reasoning* in justifying and explaining one's instructional practices and in reflecting on those practices so as to improve them; and
5. *productive disposition* toward mathematics, teaching, learning, and the improvement of practice.

In spite of the robust empirical evidence, there is no resounding consensus in the mathematics community regarding the superiority of either traditional teaching by transmission or constructivist teaching through inquiry. These terms merit brief definition here because they characterize the philosophical divide maintaining controversy within education (summarized in table 9.1) and the complexity of competing goals and multiple methods that teachers must synthesize.

A teacher-centered method merely transmits established facts and procedures to students and then measures the proficiency of recalling that knowledge

**Table 9.1.   Very Broad Comparison of Two Dominant Strands of American Pedagogy**

| Ideology | Traditional, or Classical | Progressive, or Learner-centered |
|---|---|---|
| Goal | Achievement | Development |
| Pedagogy | Transmission | Discovery/Inquiry |
| Learning process | Behaviorist | Constructivist |
|  | Information-processing | Reflection |
| Teacher role | Authoritarian | Facilitator |
| Parent role | Passive | Active |
| Student role | Passive | Active |
| Curriculum | Canonical | Contextual |
| Products | Recitation | Problem-solving |
| Governance | Autocratic | Democratic |
| Interdependence | Competitive | Cooperative |
| Culture | Homogeneous | Multicultural |
| Standards | Performance | Development |
| Student grouping | Homogeneous | Heterogeneous |
| Assessment tool | Tests | Performance |
| Theorists & practitioners | Thorndike, Skinner, Hunter, Canter, Hirsch | Dewey, Vygotsky, Piaget, Beane, McCombs, Fosnot |

Note: From Petersen, 2002.

and performing those skills. This is a simple transmission and therefore easily monitored. Standards-based reforms are associated with this approach because the objectives are clearly defined and easily measured and the teacher remains in control of the activities. Critics of the transmissionist method point out that the thinking that occurs is the teacher's, while the students remain passive recipients.

A student-centered method, however, requires student inquiry. By piquing curiosity and triggering questions, the teacher guides the student to discover meaningful patterns and connections. The deeper, unifying concepts are therefore understood instead of isolated facts and procedures. A central feature of student-centered ideology is *diversity*, that is, the great variance among students' capacities due to physical and cultural conditions often related to poverty. Few educators argue with the developmental concept of students' readiness to learn, although various theories of development (e.g. Erickson, 1950; Piaget, 1971; Vygotsky, 1978) are debated. Even fewer educators would argue with the assertion that individualizing instruction is challenging in the extreme.

Although students' physical activity may be controlled, there is far less control over what each individual perceives or concludes to be true. Thus we address an important gap between knowledge of educational psychology and teaching practices governed by imposed time structures, class sizes and compositions, and, of course, assessments. Ironically, while the federal law mandates the use of best practices defined by empirical research, the response from schools fearful of censure is to adopt practices that are not found to be most effective.

As mentioned, there are three strands of quality instruction: knowledge of students, knowledge of subject content, and knowledge of pedagogical methods. The interaction of each is more important than separate mastery. Proficiency in the first area is implied by the teacher's effective choices of combining the second and third. Nathan and Koedinger (2000, cited in Kilpatrick et al., 2001), found that "sometimes content knowledge by itself may be detrimental to good teaching. In one study, more knowledgeable teachers sometimes overestimated the accessibility of symbol-based representations and procedures" (p. 374).

The distinguishing feature is therefore the focus of thought: teachers' thoughts versus students' thoughts. As one of the project directors, Anne Brown, associate professor of mathematics at Indiana University South Bend, explained,

> The teacher looks at what the child eventually needs to know, which is ironically short-sighted. If you teach it so that the students will do well on

the exam, they may in fact do well, but they are [in trouble] when you go on beyond it, because if you teach as compartmentalized skills there is no generalized framework. They have to learn a whole new set of compartmentalized skills the next year, when in fact if they have a general structure they can take what they learned before and extend it and use it for more purposes. They will eventually have stronger tools for thinking. There is more irony because the greater efficiency in the long run is to simplify.

The greatest obstacles to implementing inquiry model instruction are teachers' mathematical and pedagogical proficiency, confounded by administrative policies supporting more directive methods and logistical challenges of meeting the needs of diverse individual students. Thus we have a knowledge-teaching gap among the teachers attempting to close the achievement gap among students.

Before proceeding to describe the development of an instrument based on the five strands of the "teaching for mathematics proficiency" model, it is important to point out one more rationale for promoting inquiry methods of teaching: there is no credible literature to the contrary claiming any other approach is superior or that inquiry is in any way detrimental. There is nonetheless another gap between knowledge and practice also at administrative and policy-making levels, thus there is a need to publicize the pattern with empirical studies reporting effects on student learning.

A companion difficulty in promoting the paradigm shift to inquiry-based standards-based methods is the need to quantify effects for the empirical research acceptable to post-NCLB policy makers. This means that a valid instrument to measure mathematics teaching proficiency would not only serve the purpose of evaluating the current project but also contribute a useful tool to the professional knowledge base. The development and validation of empirical tools is of great importance in order to determine whether the empirical findings are credible.

## MEASUREMENT TOOLS

Two survey instruments were used to evaluate three of the project goals: 1) the Conceptions of Mathematics Inventory (Grouws, Howald, and Colangelo, 1996) assessed understanding of mathematics, and 2) a new instrument, the Mathematics Teaching Profile (Petersen, Sage, Brown, and Zizzo, 2003), was developed to assess participants' tendency to teach according to the "teaching for mathematical proficiency" model, as presented by Kilpatrick, Swafford, and Findell (2001, p. 380).

The CMI assesses conceptual understanding about mathematical knowledge but not actual skills. It in no way measures mathematical understanding or conceptual understanding of mathematics. Its focus is on the person's understanding of what mathematics is as a field. Similarly, the MTP does not assess pedagogical content knowledge of mathematics but rather their views of teaching mathematics. As Brown explained,

> We wanted to look at their views about teaching mathematics. I had a strong view at the beginning that it would not make sense to try to measure how much mathematics or how much pedagogical content knowledge they could develop in the workshop because it takes YEARS to develop such knowledge, and it happens in the process of teaching your classes. The best we could hope for is that they developed a more nuanced view of what was required, so that they would seek the knowledge they need and integrate it with their teaching.

This is an important purpose, for it is related to the greater goal of continued professional development in order to cultivate quality teachers for every classroom, as anticipated by NCLB.

The original teacher version of the Conception of Mathematics Inventory (CMI) included fifty-six questions, eight for each of the seven dimensions. Two of the dimensions, status of mathematical knowledge and usefulness of mathematics, were not as helpful to the particular goals of this study as the other five dimensions. The status questions would not produce the differentiation of personal beliefs about mathematical knowledge desired nor would the usefulness questions, since the message in education about the power of mathematics is so strong that very few teachers would realistically say otherwise.

The existing eight questions from each of the remaining five themes formed the forty-item version used in the project evaluation: composition of mathematical knowledge, structure of mathematical knowledge, doing mathematics, validating ideas in mathematics, and learning mathematics. The validation of the resulting modified version of the CMI, including a factor analysis to explore and confirm the *a priori* dimensionality, was not part of this study. Rather, the focus of this report is to introduce the MTP, used here as a companion to the modified CMI.

## DEVELOPING THE MATHEMATICS TEACHING PROFILE (MTP)

Considerable rigor was used in the development of the MTP, sustained by the dialectical spirit of collaboration among the authors. The large pool of potential items were inspired by careful readings of the chapter outlining the five themes from Kilpatrick, Swafford, and Findell (2001). There followed a month of dialogue among the four authors during which ambiguity and redundancy were challenged. This not only refined the language of the items; it also contributed to the development of the workshop content, as Brown commented,

> [It was] exasperating at times: made me think hard again about what I really believed about how to explain things, what I believed about the various aspects of mathematics. You and Sara would come at me with [principles from] general education, and I'd say "No, no, math is different." [You'd ask,] "Is it like this or more like this than that?" I would have to think carefully. It made me reflect on my own practice: How I look at mathematics, how I teach, and how I teach teachers. . . . I had to think about all those things in a really practical way, to write it out in sentences.

Using the modified CMI format as an example, the 110 possible test items were reduced to eight for each of the five *a priori* conceptual strands (Kilpatrick, Swafford, and Findell, 2001) for a matching total of forty statements that would also require a ten-point Likert response (see appendix at end of chapter). Facilitating this process was a card sort activity in which each of the four authors sorted all 110 items into the five theme categories based on face validity. Frequency counts for items in each thematic collection suggested the best conceptual alignment, with three out of four occurrences considered decisively aligned. Further discussion honed categories each of the five mathematics teaching proficiency themes was expressed in eight different items (see table 9.2).

*Likert-type Scale Coding*

The original versions of the CMI used a six-point Likert-style scale, but a larger scale provides greater opportunity for differentiating patterns of response and was therefore used. For both the CMI and MTP, each test item was examined

**Table 9.2.   Alignment of MTP Items with "Teaching for Mathematical Proficiency" Model Themes**

| Theme | Mathematics Teaching Profile Items |
| --- | --- |
| Conceptual understanding | 6* 11, 16, 21, 24, 27, 30, 31* |
| Fluency | 7, 9, 15, 17, 19, 20, 33, 40 |
| Strategic competence | 4, 5, 18, 26, 28, 32, 38, 39 |
| Adaptive reasoning | 2, 3, 8, 22, 29, 35, 36, 37 |
| Productive disposition | 1, 10, 12, 13, 14, 23, 25, 34 |

Note: Items 6 and 31 were discarded due to ambiguity in scoring.

to determine whether the answer coding (0 = never true or complete dis-agreement; 9 = always true or complete agreement) was in the correct or re-verse order for a desirable answer. Desirability on the MTP was determined to be alignment with the proficiency model of teaching mathematics as defined by Kilpatrick, Swafford, and Findell (2001). When desirability order was deter-mined for both instruments, items in which a lower score was desirable were re-verse coded so that 0 = 9, 1 = 8, and so on. Two items (#6, #31) were ulti-mately discarded because the direction of desirability was ambiguous. Both were aligned with the first theme of conceptual understanding.

## Participants

Over the course of two school years, thirty-five fifth–eighth grade teachers participated. Eleven of the original participants completed all parts of the program, including multiple administrations of the two instruments. The seven remaining participants were joined by eleven new participants in the second year. This attrition and expansion complicated the statistical analysis but nonetheless provided an adequate sample to calculate internal consis-tency, a measure of reliability, and factor analysis, a way to reduce data to un-derlying constructs. Comparisons among the different groups further de-fined which items appeared to measure the greatest variance with the greatest accuracy and reliability.

## Procedure

On the first day of their first summer workshop, all thirty-five project partici-pants (n = 35) took the CMI and MTP as pre-tests online at the password-protected project website, using a code with safeguards for anonymity. Partici-pants took the post-tests at the end of the workshops and again following the one-year and two-year workshops. The interval between pre- and post-test varied from two weeks to several months.

## Data Analysis

Actual scores from were coded as Phase 1, 2, 3, and 4. Phase 1 represented all pre-test scores. Phase 2 represented all post-test scores. Phases 3 and 4 represented second and third post-tests, respectively, for the eleven partici-pants who completed both years of the project. Reliability was measured by Chronbach's Alpha. Exploratory factor analysis tested the data for dimen-sionality, using a Varimax rotation. Analysis of variance (ANOVA) was used to compare pre- and post-test scores, using a Bonferroni adjustment to control for Type I error. Data were analyzed using ANOVA for phases 1 and 2 (all pre- and post-tests, n = 28), representing participants who were in the project for one year, and then for phases 1 and 4 (n = 11), representing the participants who completed both years of the project.

## FINDINGS

### Reliability

Cronbach's Alpha for Phase 1 of the CMI was .836, indicating a high degree of reliability for the instrument. Cronbach's Alpha for Phase 1 of the MTP was .860. Both of these measures of internal consistency are in a range considered adequate for social research; therefore, the data were used to evaluate the project goals aligned with their purpose.

### Dimensionality

Although items on each instrument were grouped conceptually, dimensionality was not confirmed by factor analysis. This meant that subscale scoring

**Table 9.3. Statistically Significant Items from the MTP, Pre-Test to First Post-Test (n = 35)**

| Item | Strand | Item Wording | F | p | Effect |
|------|--------|--------------|---|---|--------|
| 11 | Conceptual Understanding | "The mathematics I know is sufficient to help me teach well at the grade level I am assigned." | 53.955 | .000** | $\eta^2=.500$ |
| 15 | Fluency | "I structure and manage effective cooperative learning activities about mathematics." | 3.613 | .063 | $\eta^2=.064$ |
| 37 | Adaptive Reasoning | "I find I understand mathematics more deeply by thinking about my students' questions and their responses to questions." | 3.927 | .053 | $\eta^2=.068$ |

Note: ** $p < .01$

**Table 9.4. Statistically Significant Items from the MTP, Pre-Test to Final Post-Test (n = 11)**

| Item | Strand | Item Wording | F | p | Effect Size |
|---|---|---|---|---|---|
| 11 | Conceptual Understanding | "The mathematics I know is sufficient to help me teach well at the grade level I am assigned." | 9.273 | .000** | $\eta^2$=.301 |
| 13 | Productive Dispositions | "I take part in professional development activities to improve my effectiveness." | 3.172 | .052 | $\eta^2$=.129 |
| 14 | Productive Dispositions | "I show my own enthusiasm about mathematics in my classroom." | 3.118 | .054 | $\eta^2$=.129 |
| 15 | Productive Dispositions | "I help students develop enthusiasm about mathematics." | 3.367 | .044 | $\eta^2$=.135 |

Note: ** $p < .01$; *$p < .05$

would not be appropriate, and individual items were therefore considered individual measures. However, the conceptual strands with which each item is associated may be helpful.

*Item Analysis*

Of interest to the grant evaluation is the statistically significant difference in item scores in between pre- and post-tests (see tables 9.3 and 9.4). Only one item of the thirty-eight was statistically significant in comparison to the first post-test and the last post-test: #11 ("The mathematics I know is sufficient to help me teach well at the grade level I am assigned"). However, the strength of the difference declined: the F statistic dropped from a robust 53.955 to 9.273, although the p value remained nil.

The effect size ($\eta^2$ = .500) also declined ($\eta2$ = .301). In addition to item #11, only two items, 15 and 37, demonstrated statistically significant change from pre-test to first post-test for all participants administered at the conclusion of the summer workshop. Also in addition to 11, three others—13, 14, and 25—were significantly different for the eleven participants who completed both years of the project from their pre-test to the final post-test at the end of the second year.

## DISCUSSION

The internal consistency of the Mathematics Teaching Profile (MTP) is certainly adequate ($\alpha > .8$). Current statistical theory, however, advocates the use of the standard error of measurement (SEM) to indicate reliability (Chronbach and Shavelson, 2004). The SEM is the square root of the error variance, reporting the degree of uncertainty about the individuals' responses. "The figure is often surprisingly large" (p. 410), but it requires larger samples. Further use of the instrument and subsequent psychometric study of it may provide the opportunity to calculate the standard error of measurement with greater confidence.

The small number of statistically significant items may be due at least in part to the small sample sizes (Thomspon, 2005). However, these small results are still worthwhile in that the two items found significant both relate to a move away from a strictly procedural understanding of mathematics (e.g., distinct formulas are all that one needs to know) to a more conceptual understanding. For this project, it is unlikely that an instrument would show large gains in mathematical knowledge. However, there is some meaningful interpretation possible.

The MTP was developed to assess the five strands of the "teaching for mathematical proficiency" model. Although the dimensionality of the instrument did not confirm the strands as reliable subscales, the items are nonetheless associated with different *a priori* themes. Different techniques of factor analysis may render a simple structure that could then be used to test the theoretical model proposed by Kilpatrick and colleagues (2001). Another factor analytic exercise to be conducted is to analyze the CMI and MTP data as one combined instrument in hope that a simple structure will emerge. This has a logical support in that both have interest in conceptual understanding and practical applications, although one is ostensibly focused on the content area and the other on the teaching of it.

Interestingly enough, the conceptual understanding thread was reduced by the removal of two items too ambiguous to score meaningfully, but another of its items emerged as the most robust of the remaining thirty-eight. There was one item each from the fluency (#15) and adaptive reasoning (#37) strands that while statistically significant were nonetheless very weak ($\eta^2 = .064$ and $\eta^2 = .068$ respectively). In addition to #11, there were three statistically significant items in the comparison to the first and last post-tests, and they were all associated with the productive dispositions strand. None of the items from the strategic competence strand emerged as statistically significant.

It must be noted that, given that the dimensionality was not confirmed through the initial exploratory factor analysis and that the search for a new simple structure was not a part of this study, further study may yield different constructs than the *a priori* terms used here. Although it would be tempting to conclude that the MTP is therefore reliable for measuring changes in conceptual understanding and productive disposition, there are rival hypotheses. In spite of the exhaustive effort to generate appropriate items, the instrument may simply feature no items that adequately assess the less represented strands. Another possibility is that the workshop had little effect, which invites a discussion of the quality of the workshop, a topic beyond the scope of this article. The interest here, though, is in the quality of the instrument itself. At this preliminary stage of developing the instrument, it is prudent to point out that although constructed and analyzed with all due respect for the conventions of survey research, the instrument requires more extensive use and analysis to become more than promising. If further investigation does uphold its reliability and better describe the nature of the items, it could be very useful for assessing professional development toward the use of inquiry model best practices, and it could be used to quantify the degree of adherence to the inquiry-based pedagogical ideology and thereby correlate ideology to student achievement. If the simple structure is adequately robust, the subscales could be administered separately, perhaps in the context of professional development activities related to each one. Finally, the instrument could be used as its name implies, as a descriptive profile, for teachers' reflective practice, similar to self-report measures of constructivism.

In summary, the Mathematics Teaching Profile is introduced here as a measure of teacher quality that may serve the profession's continuing commitment to closing the gaps between theory and practice, between knowledge and teaching, and, indirectly, the achievement gap among students. Regarding the collaboration between the Department of Mathematical Sciences and the School of Education during the Mathematical Proficiency through Inquiry-Based Teaching and Learning project, the construction of the instrument fostered shared understanding of the content area and certainly contributed a helpful perspective.

## REFERENCES

American Association for the Advancement of Science. (1989). *Science for all Americans: A Project 2061 Report on literacy goals in science, mathematics, and technology.* Washington, DC: Author.

Ausubel, A. (1968). *Educational psychology: A cognitive view.* New York: Holt, Rinehart & Winston.

Bransford, J., Brown, A., and Cocking, R. (Eds.). (1999). *How people learn: Brain, mind, experience, and school.* National Research Council. Washington, DC: National Academies Press. Retrieved from www.nap.edu/html/howpeople1/index.html

Bruner, J. (1950). "Social psychology and group processes." *Annual Review of Psychology,* *1,* 119–51.

Chronbach, R., and Shavelson, R. (2004). "My current thoughts on coefficient alpha and successor procedures." *Educational and Psychological Measurement, 64,* 391–406.

Erikson, E. (1950). *Childhood and society.* Norton.

Gardner, H. (1972). *The quest for mind.* New York: Harper.

Grouws, D. A., Howald, C. L. & Colangelo, N. (1996, April). *Student conceptions of mathematics: A comparison of mathematically talented students and typical high school algebra students.* Paper presented at the annual meeting of the American Educational Research Association, New York.

Jackson, A. (1997). "The math wars: California battles it out over mathematics education reform (Part I)." *Notices of the AMS, 4,* 695–702.

Kilpatrick J., Swafford J., and Findell, B. (Eds.). (2001). *Adding it up: Helping children learn mathematics.* Washington, DC: National Academies Press.

Ma, L. (1999). *Knowing and teaching elementary mathematics: Teachers' understanding of fundamental mathematics in China and the United States (Studies in mathematical thinking and learning).* Mahwah, NJ: Erlbaum.

National Council of Teachers of Mathematics (NCTM). (1989). *Curriculum and evaluation standards for school mathematics.* Reston, VA: Author.

Petersen, N. J. (2002). *The Classroom Educator Role Profile (CERP): A psychometric investigation of a teacher belief survey.* Doctoral dissertation. Seattle: Pacific University.

Petersen, N. J., Sage, S. M., Brown, A., and Zizzo, P. (2003). *Mathematics Teaching Profile.* Unpublished instrument, Indiana University South Bend.

Phillips, D. C. (1997). "How, why, what, when, and where: Perspectives on constructivism in psychology and education." *Issues in Education, 3,* 151–94.

Piaget, J. (1971). *Genetic epistemology.* Norton.

Sage, S. M., and Petersen, N. J. (2005). "Mathematical proficiency through inquiry-based teaching and learning: Final report 2003–2005. Improving Teacher Quality Project number: 02-03 Indiana University South Bend." Submitted to the Indiana Board of Higher Education May 27, 2005.

Shulman, L.S. (1987). "Knowledge and teaching: Foundations of the new reform." *Harvard Educational Review, 57,* 1–22.

Star, J. R., and Hoffmann, A. J. (forthcoming). "Assessing the impact of standards-based curricula: Investigating students' epistemological conceptions of mathematics." *The Mathematics Educator.*

Thompson, B. (2005). *Exploratory and confirmatory factor analysis.* Washington, DC: American Psychological Association/Erlbaum.

von Glasersfeld, E. (1997). "Amplification of a constructivist perspective." *Issues in Education, 3,* 203–10.

Vygotsky, L. S. (1930/1978). *Mind in society: The development of the higher psychological processes.* Cambridge, MA: The Harvard University Press.

Winerip, M. (2005). "Study great ideas, but teach to the test." *New York Times.* July 13, 2005. Retrieved August 12, 2005, from www.nytimes.com/2005/07/13/education/13education.html?ex=1122091200&en=0a09ad889eb0d7a5&ei=5070.

## APPENDIX: MATHEMATICS TEACHING PROFILE (MTP) WITH ONLINE INSTRUCTIONS (PETERSEN, BROWN, SAGE, AND ZIZZO, 2003)

Instructions: In this survey, you are asked to indicate how often the given statement is true about your teaching practice. Assign each statement a value from **0** to **9**. The scale runs from **0** indicating it is never true about your teaching practice to **9** indicating that it is always true about your practice. For statements that are sometimes true and sometimes not, the intermediate values allow you indicate how often the statement is true. Click on the button to the left of the desired value for each statement.

1. I look for more ways to understand my students' mathematical thinking.
2. I explain to students, parents, and others why I choose to organize my lessons the way I do.
3. I review student work carefully to examine the need to re-teach a particular mathematics concept.
4. Once I understand a student's mathematical difficulty, I can help the student overcome it.
5. I revise my mathematics lessons "on the spot" if students are having difficulty with my first approach.
6. There are some mathematical ideas that I understand but do not know how to teach to my students.
7. I apply several strategies for encouraging students to reveal their mathematical thinking.
8. I like to talk to colleagues about students' misconceptions so that I can get another perspective.
9. During instruction, I assess my students' ability to correctly carry out mathematical procedures.
10. I find that there is a lot more to learn about how people learn mathematics.
11. The mathematics I know is sufficient to help me teach well at the grade level I am assigned.
12. I analyze my curriculum materials and consider how to maximize their effectiveness for learning.
13. I take part in professional development activities to improve my effectiveness as a mathematics teacher.
14. I show my own enthusiasm about mathematics in my classroom.
15. I structure and manage effective cooperative learning activities about mathematics.

16. I need to know more about how students in grades 5–8 actually learn mathematics.
17. I structure and manage effective whole-class discussions about mathematics.
18. I use teaching strategies that encourage students to think about and use their prior knowledge of mathematics.
19. I use one or more routines for responding to wrong answers during class discussion.
20. I apply a variety of techniques for teaching the mathematical ideas in my curriculum.
21. I need to know more about how to teach mathematics to children in grades 5–8.
22. I spend time reflecting on my mathematics lessons after I teach them.
23. I let my students see that I am still learning about mathematics and about teaching.
24. There are different strategies for teaching different mathematics content.
25. I help students develop enthusiasm about mathematics.
26. I design instructional tasks that are effective in helping my students learn the intended mathematics topic.
27. I know why my students have difficulty with certain mathematical ideas.
28. For each lesson, I have clear objectives that are based on mathematics standards.
29. I tend to encourage my students to offer their ideas, and then as a group we resolve any confusion that arises.
30. I know how my teaching improves my students' mathematical proficiency.
31. There are some mathematical ideas that I understand but do not know how students learn them.
32. I use students' mathematical ideas to help the whole class learn.
33. During instruction I assess my students' understanding of mathematical concepts.
34. One way I learn more about teaching mathematics is by analyzing what goes on in my classroom.
35. I review the mathematical work of a particular student to assess his or her strengths and weaknesses.
36. I think my students learn best if I demonstrate how to solve problems first and then coach them while they practice.
37. I find I understand mathematics more deeply by thinking about my students' questions and their responses to questions.

38. When planning, I emphasize preparing my students for the mathematics they will learn next year.
39. There are opportunities in my classroom for students to use multiple representations of mathematics.
40. During instruction I respond effectively to my students' mathematical questions.

*III*

# DIVERSITY, TEACHING, AND LEARNING

# "Can You Spare Some Social Change?": Preparing New Teachers to Teach Social Justice in Times of Educational Reform and Standardized Curriculum

## Finney Cherian

*The chapter explores the complexity and importance of guiding teacher candidates to take up anti-oppressive curricula such as social justice and equity in their classroom practices, a task many educators report made difficult in an era of education reform and standardized curriculum. This is further complicated by the fact that often discussions on social justice and teacher education are heavily populated with philosophical abstractions and academic jargon, leaving many classroom teachers uninspired. For this reason, this chapter offers a discussion of social justice and initial teacher education which is theoretical, visionary, and rich with classroom examples.*

> "Every social actor knows a great deal about the conditions of reproduction of the society of which he or she is a member."
> (Giddens, 1979, p. 5)

### INTRODUCTION

The intention of this chapter is to share ways to help teacher candidates deepen their understanding of social justice curricula and critical teaching. It is hoped that other teacher educators will be encouraged to reflect upon new possibilities for helping teacher candidates create classrooms devoted to democratic education, social justice, and equity. The ideas presented here come from struggles I have faced in the last five years as a teacher educator working with U.S. and Canadian teacher candidates to have teacher candidates enter the profession prepared to confront social inequalities and highly qualified to teach academic knowledge, with the conviction that all children regardless of social circumstance and ethnicity can learn.

During a language arts methods class, two of my teacher candidates expressed the following sentiments: "My associate teacher does not want me to teach any issues of social justice in student teaching. She says the curriculum doesn't have room for that stuff. If teachers don't want us to teach social justice, maybe what you're teaching is unrealistic." Another student chimed in, "There is nothing on the Praxis teacher test we have to take on social justice. I want to focus on things that will be on the test." The procrustean bed of the accountability and standards-based movement that had begun to cut away at K–12 classrooms had begun to hack at my legs and the ethos of my course.

## A MISSING PIECE IN SCHOOL IMPROVEMENT

The behemoth of the standards-based curricula movement has rumbled across the landscape of education. Local boards of education have been pressured to keep abreast of new curriculum frameworks and accountability requirements. Administrators, teachers, educational researchers, and parent groups sit in opposing camps fractured over the question, "What should students know and be able to do?" Albeit, not a new question in curriculum inquiry, it is one which has become more problematic in a climate of high-stakes testing and accountability. For many, hope is long overdue in education, especially for minority students whose progress continues to languish in comparison to White middle-class populations (Lewis, 2000). Regardless of what legislative reforms are in vogue, minority groups continue to exist at the margins of classroom life, forced to play supporting roles far from center stage.

Ironically, while many in education harshly critique reforms like the No Child Left Behind Act (NCLB) of 2001, the essence of the act seeks to address the same issues that equity and justice advocates have tried to address for years, namely protecting schools in poorer communities from the placement of uncertified teachers (Poplin and Rivera, 2005). While we all want accountability, the tensions with current accountability reforms can be traced back to the following: its form and manner of implementation, effectiveness in relation to meeting its objectives, congruence to our democratic ideals, and receptiveness to critique by those it governs (our teachers) and those it serves (our children). I believe the children of the nation are better served, if those in the field of education and legislators can get beyond the quagmire of accountability debates and focus on co-shaping and evolving the system for better achievement outcomes.

Ryan (2002) suggests, "The evaluation community has the responsibility and obligation to go beyond position papers to play an integral part in the study of, improvement of, and judgments about the merit and worth of these assessment and accountability systems" (p. 453). Assessment and measurement scholars need to identify the exact shape and substance of evaluation's relationship to accountability and the broader issues of bias, equity, reliability, and validity. These issues merit their own discussion and exceed the focus of this chapter. However, Ryan (2002) offers a detailed discussion on the merits and shortcomings of evaluation scholarship in co-shaping current accountability reforms.

I believe one missing piece in school improvement is the lack of focus on critical teaching, a concept which has been much neglected but an indispensable element in the quest for democratic and socially responsive education.

## CRITICAL TEACHING DEFINED

What is critical teaching? Shor (1992) offers one of the clearest definitions in the literature. Its attributes are a student-centered program for multicultural democracy in school and society that approaches individual growth as an active, cooperative, and social process.

Critical teaching involves thinking, reading, and writing that go beyond the cuticle layers of dominant myths and social practices. It is teaching in line with the traditions of Foucault (1980) and Freire (1997), which liberate subjugated histories and power from the hegemonic structures and practices of dominant cultures (Giroux and McLaren, 1986). It is a commitment on the part of teachers to use the different subject disciplines (math, language, social studies, etc.) to get students to deeply critique the existing social order, asking of themselves—What is the relationship of my beliefs and social condition to those of my fellow citizens? By raising such questions, teachers can guide students to de-center themselves and break out of the confinements of privatism and self-regard (Green, 1995). All of us must consider the fact that we are not agents who merely observe social order; we participate within, and some are pushed to the fringes of it. Therefore, its current and future condition is of importance to all. Thus, teachers and students need to be driven by a vision to use their knowledge and skills toward the liberation of the oppressed (Kauchak and Eggen, 2003).

## STAND-ALONE CULTURAL DIVERSITY COURSES

Throughout North America, school populations have become more linguistically and culturally diverse, while teaching populations have remained mainly White, middle class, and female (Sleeter, 1998). Brown (2004) reports that by the year 2010, census extrapolations predict that 95 percent of K–12 classroom teachers will be White middle-class females who will have had limited cross-cultural experiences. In order to address this incongruity in cultural frames of reference, numerous faculties of education have implemented stand-alone cultural diversity courses. However, stand-alone diversity courses have the propensity to become exactly that—stand-alone. In the minds of teacher candidates, their content and purpose appear abstract and irrelevant to the real skills and knowledge gained in traditional core methodology courses (Brown, 2004).

The intent of these courses has been to reinforce the importance of validating cultural diversity and student needs in the hopes that education becomes an equitable enterprise for all. However, Brown (2004) reports that teacher candidates enter and exit stand-alone cultural courses unchanged, maintaining the many cultural stereotypes they held prior to the program. Banks (1995) and Irvine (1992) (as cited in Brown, 2004) attribute this stasis in cultural attitudes to resistance and resentment to multicultural doctrine, instruction, and application. Many teacher candidates report that while they receive adequate exposure to sociocultural theory, little is provided in the way of helping them implement such pedagogies into their daily classroom work (Solomon and Allen, 2001). This circumstance becomes more problematic if other methods courses don't take up or focus on cultural issues in their activities and content. In addition, if teacher candidates are not given an opportunity to work with mentors who model mastery and reverence for socially conscious pedagogies they remain at the level of ideals.

The totality of these circumstances leads many teachers to see anti-oppressive pedagogy as merely theoretical abstractions and the stand-alone cultural diversity courses which contextualize these discourses, as cul-de-sacs which make no in-roads into the daily realities of K–12 school life. Hence, the applicability and merits of critical teaching in subjects such as social justice tumbles into the abyss of the theory-practice divide. This, in turn, translates to the sentiments raised by my students—"maybe what you're teaching is unrealistic" and "there is nothing on the Praxis teacher test we have to take on social justice. I want to focus on things that will be on the test."

The effectiveness of stand-alone cultural diversity classes can be greatly enhanced if other instructional methodology courses create significant space to raise cultural-cognizance, sensitivity, and commitment to social justice. The issues of social justice need to be developed as a shared vision through the entire depth and breadth of initial teacher education programs. This is the most effective way to narrow the theory-practice divide: by allowing teacher candidates to see how cross-curricular standards, resources, and teaching methods can be used to advance social justice while helping to develop academic skills in their K–12 students (Garmon, 2004).

## TRANSFORMATIVE INTELLECTUALS OR TECHNICIANS?

One major concern for faculties of education is to balance the internal desire of their academics to maintain the intellectual freedom of their courses against the external pressures of teacher testing and various standards-based practices changing the content and vision of their courses. I believe there will come a time when the national accreditation reviews of faculties of education will be correlated to the performance of exiting graduates on teacher tests. So, do we succumb to these pressures and solely focus on producing technicians who can dutifully execute the wishes of outside agencies and get high marks on exit exams, technicians who will operate in a closed system of legislated curriculum, unable to exercise internal critique? I propose we help prepare our students to meet current reform benchmarks but also work toward the benchmarks of Dewey (1938) and Schön (1983) who sought reflective practitioners proficient in critiquing self and system as transformative intellectuals.

Drawing upon the work of Giroux and McLaren (1986), transformative intellectuals can be defined in the following manner:

1. They take into account questions of language, culture, race, and the ways in which they affect a student's academic and social outcomes. A student's family, cultural, and economic background should never be seen as impediments to learning or nor should they be pathologized as such.
2. They critique curriculum and introduce material that allows students to see their lives outside of school reflected in school, along with their cultural and linguistic heritage.
3. They vigorously endeavor to understand the implications of all forms of oppression in their students' lives. They explore every aspect of the relationship between culture, politics, economics, and contemporary schooling.
4. They see themselves as agents who are politically and morally protective of the histories, knowledge, and experiences that define their students.

While I believe that faculties of education can adopt the education reforms taking place, our efforts to adapt to reforms must not compromise the democratic governance of schools. Democratic ideals cannot be maintained by uncritical technicians who compromise, yielding to every trend and whim of the state (Solomon and Allen, 2001).

## ENCOUNTERING OTHERS THROUGH
## COMMUNITY AND INQUIRY

The following three "Rs" need to exist in teacher development: Revisit, Rehearsal, and Refashion (Britzman, 1991). In my language arts methods courses, I create opportunities for teacher candidates to revisit their own personal autobiographies in schools. They need time and opportunity to rehearse their new skills and emerging identities as educators. And finally, drawing upon the first two Rs, they need to envision new possibilities for improving their classroom practices and relationship to students. I start with the "self" and then move outward to the "other," in the hopes of addressing the following paradox: the learning of social justice needs to begin with helping teacher candidates to value their personal cultural identities, beliefs, and lived experiences but then help them transcend themselves and embrace the identities, beliefs, and narratives of others.

This is the essence of community committed to caring and inquiry. To accomplish these goals, we need to assist teacher candidates to reflect upon the following: (1) their personhood as educators, (2) their sense of connectedness to others through the sharing of personal narratives, and (3) the politics of their social location in relation to fellow citizens marginalized by society.

### We Teach from Our Personhood

Classrooms are places where competing and conflicting selfhoods reside. As teacher educators, we must not only insist that teacher candidates master content knowledge and sound teaching practice (the objectivism) but also that they explore how their individual autobiographies interact with others and the world (Palmer, 1998). The two activities described help share and listen to the stories of others. Cohen (1998) identifies three key ideas about story as the conduit for building a caring community of learners:

1. Every person has a story to tell; respectful listening elicits the stories that need to be told.
2. We shape the meaning of our experiences through the telling of stories; we honor each other's stories by responding to them.
3. Community grows stronger when all its stories are celebrated. The celebration stitches a fabric of human caring. (p. 53)

### A Sense of Connectedness

During the first weeks of school, I would provide each teacher candidate with a large sheet of Bristol board cut in the shape of a puzzle piece. Having prepared the pieces, I ensured that each puzzle piece interlocked and fit with another Bristol board section. The interlocking pieces symbolized the uniqueness and interconnectedness found in our classroom community. I always pointed out to the class that each piece in a jigsaw helps to create a complete picture. Thus, the absence of one member of our class, like a missing puzzle piece, would diminish the class community from being complete. As students decorated and personalized their pieces, I would staple them to the bulletin boards that surrounded the class. On each puzzle piece, the students were encouraged to mount family photos. Each puzzle piece also had a large Zip-Lock freezer bag glued to it so as to hold any special articles which held sentimental value to the student.

One year I had a student named Chris, who displayed a photocopy of the first paycheck his grandfather received in America as he emigrated from Poland. On his 3x5 description card, he wrote about the times his grandfather would show him the framed paycheck, which was a symbol of a poor Polish farm boy's dream of coming to America and having a better life. Liz, another teacher candidate, mounted a handkerchief fragranced with Estee Lauder's perfume Beautiful, her mother's favorite scent. A single parent African-American woman who put three children through college working as a hotel chamber maid and waitress, Liz's mother had recently died of breast cancer. On her puzzle piece, Liz described how she would spray her mother's favorite scent on a handkerchief, which she would pull out and inhale deeply in times of fear or self-doubt. The fragrance brought a sense of her mother's presence into the moment, giving Liz courage to carry on. Over the course of the first few weeks, I would have students interview one another about their puzzle pieces. The classroom was filled with artifacts, tears, and laughter. By the end of the first few weeks, a group of strangers from different walks of life and experiences had become implicated in each other's lives through their stories, beliefs, and aspirations.

*Politics of Location*

Dialogue poems are written and read by two people. Each partner creates a response based on the statements of the other writer. To begin the activity, I show my student teachers a picture of a well-known wealthy individual. In the following example, I have used a picture of billionaire Bill Gates. Along with my language arts teacher candidates, we brainstorm and record what we would say to him if he were to enter the room. I also have them list the ways his life is different from their own. Next, I show them a picture of a homeless person and have them repeat what they did with the Gates picture. Once we have exhausted their questions and thoughts about the homeless person, we work in pairs. One person takes on the voice of the billionaire, the second the voice of the home-less person. Students draw on their individual work to create a dialogue poem based on what they believe the billionaire and the homeless man would say if they had a chance to meet and talk to one another. Interestingly, in the years I have done this activity no one has made the voice of the billionaire empathetic. It is usually one of indifference to the plight of the homeless person. Such ob-servations are very telling about the assumptions my student teachers hold about the wealthy and the homeless of North America. Below is the partner poem en-titled "The Tale of Two Bills" created by undergraduate teacher candidates:

| *Reader 1* | *Reader 2* |
|---|---|
| I see the world through high speed cable. | I see the world from the sidewalk. |
| I have a hard drive. | I have a hard life! |
| Everyone knows my name and face. | People see me every day and pretend they don't see me. |
| I have many homes. I'm Billionaire Bill Gates. | I am homeless but not nameless. My name is Bill like yours. |

Reading this poem, the reader cannot help but be drawn to the wonder-ful declaration that "homeless is not nameless." Such gems are what we want our teacher candidates to unearth as they go into the classroom prepared to teach an empathetic curriculum.

## FUTURE DIRECTIONS

Schools of education cannot instill the social justice message alone. Strong partnership and shared vision is required with local K–12 schools, teachers, and administrators. One way this can be done is through Professional Development Schools (PDS). Throughout North America, many researchers have focused on the implications for situating teacher education within new partnerships with schools that have adopted teacher education as a central part of their mission statement (Cochran-Smith and Lytle, 1993; Darling-Hammond, 1993; Holmes Group, 1990). Review of the role and effectiveness of PDS schools indicates that such structures offer faculties of education a critical mass of educators committed to areas like social justice and equity pedagogies (Duquette, 1996). It is of great importance that teacher candidates have skilled mentors who can guide them in implementing the theoretical aspects of critical pedagogy into their daily classroom work.

With respect to the evolution of the core curriculum and practices of faculties of education, Poplin and Rivera (2005) list key issues in helping teacher candidates seek social justice and accountability:

1. Increasing candidates of color into faculties of teacher education.
2. Partnering with schools that are closing the achievement gaps so that candidates are placed with effective teachers in effective schools. Hiring those teachers to help instruct our candidates.
3. Emphasizing knowledge, understanding, and creativity in teaching and assessing the curriculum standards in multiple ways with all students.
4. Teaching teachers how schools have perpetuated the achievement gap and other social inequities and how these may be overcome.
5. Inspiring teachers with the details of schools that are eliminating achievement gaps.
6. Encouraging teachers to develop the attitudes and dispositions necessary to do the hard work to help all students achieve.
7. Focusing the work during the program on teaching and documenting their students' progress.
8. Broadly educating teacher candidates by addressing both sides of the aforementioned paradoxes and diverse ideologies. (p. 35)

## CONCLUSION

While many Americans continue to ideologically embrace the single voice of *e pluribus unum*, voices from other Americans claiming their identities defiantly yell, "I am Black, Chicano, Chinese, Indian, Aboriginal, White, queer, straight, female, male, rich, homeless, Christian, Muslim, and Jew." As a democratic multicultural country, we must recognize that we are forever in a struggle to balance the needs of the individual against the needs of the community. The goal is not to speak with one voice, but to create compassionate spaces in our classrooms where all voices are audible and allowed to maintain their distinct timbre (Fox, 1993). How do we work toward such an end?

The teaching of social justice is a delicate and dangerous proposition. Courage is required to teach and learn from such a perspective. It is a pedagogical perspective that requires the teachers and students to see themselves as the curriculum of study. Educators of social justice and equity must commit themselves to creating classroom activities that assist their students to value and advocate not only for their own needs but also for those of others. We must help them to develop an unquenchable thirst to care for others. To work toward this sense of caring for others, Solomon and Allen (2001) recommend faculties consider the following:

1. Provide an environment in which teacher candidates of various social identities (race, ethnicity, gender, sexual orientation, exceptionality, social class, etc.) have extended opportunities to develop teaching competencies and build professional relationships in a collaborative manner.
2. Integrate issues of equity, social justice, and diversity into the curriculum and pedagogy of teacher education scholarship and the classrooms of practicum schools.
3. Develop collaboration among practicum school staff, representatives of community organizations, teacher candidates, and their teacher educators, forming a community of learners. (p. 222)

Finally, teaching social justice requires teachers to envision their students and themselves as truth seekers prepared to act on their knowledge to change societal inequalities. History has proven that activism and resistance are means through which social change moves. To expose inequity and not encourage change for those conditions promotes apathy. Peterson (1994) writes, "apathy is not OK. At times when cynicism and hopelessness increasingly dominate our youth, helping students understand the world and their relationship to it by encouraging social action may be one of the few antidotes" (p. 38). The victims of a society hold the critique of their society. They cry in the words of feminist poet Lillian Allen (1993), "Can you spare some social change?"

## REFERENCES

Allen, L. (1993). *Women do this everyday*. Toronto: Women's Press.

Britzman, D. (1991). *Practice makes practice: Critical study of learning to teach*. New York: State University of New York Press.

Brown, E. L. (2004). "What precipitates change in cultural awareness during a multicultural course: The message or the method?" *Journal of Teacher Education, 55*(4), 325–40.

Cochran-Smith, M., and Lytle, S. L. (Eds.). (1993). *Inside/outside: Teacher research and knowledge*. New York: Teachers College Press.

Cohen, C. (1998). "The true colors of the new Jim Toomey: Transformation, integrity, trust in *Educating teachers about oppression*." In E. Lee, D. Menkart, and M. Okazawa-Rey (Eds.), *Beyond heroes and holidays: A practical guide to K-12 anti-racist, multicultural education and staff development*. Washington, DC: Network of Educators on the Americas.

Darling-Hammond, L. (Ed.). (1993). *Professional development schools*. New York: Teachers College Press.

Dewey, J. (1938). *Experience and Education*. New York: Collier Books.

Duquette, C. (1996). "Partnerships in preservice education: Perspectives of associate teachers and student teachers." *McGill Journal of Education, 3*(1), 59–81.

Freire, P. (1997). *Pedagogy of the oppressed*. New York: Continuum Publishing.

Foucault, M. (1980). *Power/knowledge*. Ed. C. Gordon. New York: Pantheon.

Fox, M. (1993). *Radical reflections: Passionate opinions on teaching, learning and living*. New York: Harcourt Brace and Company.

Garmon, M. A. (2004). "Changing preservice teachers' attitudes/beliefs about diversity: What are the critical factors?" *Journal of Teacher Education, 55*(3), 201–13.

Giddens, A. (1979). *Central problems in social theory: Action, structure and contradiction in social analysis*. Berkeley: University of California Press.

Giroux, H., and McLaren, P. (1986). "Teacher education and the politics of engagement: The case for democratic schooling." *Harvard Educational Review, 56*(3), 213–38.

Greene, M. (1995). *Releasing the imagination*. San Francisco: Jossey-Bass.

Holmes Group. (1990). *Tomorrow's schools: Principles for the design of professional development schools*. East Lansing, MI: The Holmes Group.

Kauchak, D. P., and Eggen, P. D. (2003). *Learning and teaching: Research-based methods*. Boston: Allyn and Bacon.

Lewis, A. C. (2000). "The notorious G-A-P." *Phi Delta Kappan, 82*(2), 103–4.

Palmer, P. J. (1998). *The courage to teach: Exploring the inner landscape of a teacher's life*. San Francisco: Jossey-Bass.

Peterson, B. (1994). "Teaching for social justice: One teacher's journey." In *Rethinking Our Classrooms: Teaching for equity and justice*. Milwaukee, WI: Rethinking Schools.

Poplin, M., and Rivera, J. (2005). "Merging social justice and accountability: Educating qualified and effective teachers." *Theory into Practice, 44*(1), 27–37.

Ryan, K. (2002). "Shaping educational accountability systems." *American Journal of Evaluation, 23*(4), 453–68.

Schön, D. (1983). *The reflective practitioner: How professionals think in action*. New York: Basic Books.

Shor, I. (1992). *Empowering education: Critical teaching for social change*. Chicago: University of Chicago Press.

Sleeter, C. (1998). "Teaching whites about racism." In E. Lee, D. Menkart, and M. Okazawa-Rey (Eds.), *Beyond heroes and holidays: A practical guide to K–12 anti-racist, multicultural education and staff development*. Washington, DC: Network of Educators on the Americas.

Solomon, R. P., and Allen, A. M. A. (2001). "The struggle for equity, diversity, and social justice in teacher education." In J. P. Portelli and R. P. Solomon (Eds.), *The erosion of democracy in education: From critique to possibilities*. Calgary: Detselig Enterprises.

# Integrating Multicultural Themes with Content Area Subjects

## *Karen Bolak*

*Educational research reveals that most teachers have limited exposure to diverse popula-tions. Students' ethnic background, economic status, gender, sexual orientation, language, race, and abilities affect how students relate to peers and teachers. This chapter empha-sizes that student success is often related to teachers' application of multicultural educa-tional concepts in their classrooms.*

## INTRODUCTION: CULTURAL DIVERSITY IN THE SCHOOLS

Educators in the United States need more than a content area subject knowl-edge base to teach students. They also need a cultural knowledge base and an understanding of their students, regardless of their students' gender, sexual ori-entation, social class, religious, ethnic, or racial identity. Sleeter (2001) reports that it is "widely recognized that the cultural gap between children in the schools and teachers is large and growing" (p. 94). This widening cultural gap between teachers and students is of the utmost concern to a professor of edu-cation at a Midwestern university. Thus, the professor designed an assignment that required graduate students to understand and infuse their students' cultural identities across content areas, using multicultural premises.

The professor's concern for this cultural divide is intensified by demo-graphics. Parkay and Stanford (2004) inform educators that in 2000, "39 per-cent of public school students were considered to be part of a minority group. . . . It is projected that by 2025 half of U.S. youth will be white and half will be minority" (p. 241). Given this projection, and the existence of the cultural gap between students and teachers, every professor must claim responsibility for teaching teachers to become advocates for students of all cultural backgrounds.

Practicing teachers must understand their students' backgrounds and promote learning opportunities for all youngsters, through engagement as well as inclusive curricula, regardless of their culture. The purpose of this chapter is to highlight inspirational themes from literature related to this important topic, describe the assignment, present examples from the assignment, and report how university students responded to the assignment.

## INSPIRATION AND STRATEGIES: INFLUENCING THEMES FOUND IN LITERATURE

Several themes that relate to teaching and learning found in educational literature served as inspiration to the professor and the university students. These concepts are related to the gap between teachers and students and include the effect of children's socioeconomic status, race, cultural, and ethnic background on their schooling experiences. There are multiple factors that produce the gap. Language is one of the most prominent influences.

Vasquez (1996) points out that "Language is part of the glue that helps us make meaning of life. Thus, language is a critical element in eliminating the mistreatment of any group" (p. 14). More often than not, teachers are insensitive to the fact that one's culture is embedded in language. Parkay and Stanford (2004) state, "Bilingual education is designed to help students maintain their ethnic identity and become proficient in both English and the language of the home" (p. 243). Because teachers from the dominant culture may not understand the implications of their own cultural identity (including language) on learning, they have difficulty understanding the importance of language as a part of their students' formal educational experience. Language also carries power and influence:

> We must not use language to set one human community and its symbols over another and we must especially remain ever aware that the same power of language that brings us to the gates of divinity has been used to dehumanize. . . . We must come to understand that language . . . [has the] power to draw us together in community—especially through sharing. . . . So too [it has] the power of destruction." (Green, 1992, p. 136)

Green's writing demonstrates that exclusion of students based upon language of origin can have a devastating potential for school children as well as society. Further, Nieto (2004) broadens the discussion:

> Multicultural education is a transformative process that goes far beyond cultural and linguistic maintenance. In the final analysis, multicultural education needs to confront not just issues of difference but also issues of power and privilege in society. This means challenging racism and other biases as well as the inequitable structures, policies and practices of schools and, ultimately, of society itself. (p. xxvii)

Moreover, Nieto encourages teachers to consider that no student should have to make a choice between family (belonging) and school (succeeding). Teachers must acknowledge and validate each student's rich personal history.

The varied experiences of others should be made visible in our schools and curricula. Students' culture is part of who they are as individuals and must be validated by their teachers. Thus, Vasquez (1996), Nieto (2004), Green (1992), and Parkay and Stanford (2004) made available the inspiration for the assignment.

Banks (2005) provided the instructional multicultural dimensions that could be used as strategies for the planning portion of the assignment. He suggests that educators use five dimensions for inclusive multicultural practices in education. If students consider and utilize the strategies when planning, the teachers will become more culturally competent educators. Banks's (2005) dimensions are below:

- Content Integration (using examples, generalizations, and theories from other cultures that are related to the subject area being studied)
- The Knowledge Construction Process (helping students understand how cultural assumptions and biases have an impact on how knowledge is constructed)
- An Equity Pedagogy (the modification of teaching techniques to consider the variety of styles that are found within various socioeconomic, racial, gender, cultural, and ethnic groups of students)
- Prejudice Reduction (raising student awareness and changing attitudes by teaching about racism and racially prejudiced behaviors)
- An Empowering School Culture and Social Structure (creation of a school culture that empowers and includes students across racial, ethnic, and gender groups)

Teachers have the ability to transform procedures, instructional practices, and curricula in the schools. Therefore, educators have the potential to be advocates for youth promoting improvement for all children.

## CURRENT STATE OF AFFAIRS: WHY TEACHERS' PERCEPTIONS DEMAND ATTENTION

During the first day of class, entitled "The Diverse Learner and the Curriculum," graduate students (most of who are practicing teachers) are asked: Why do you think you are required to take a course about curriculum development for the diverse learner? In summary, the majority of students report to the instructor that they are certified, licensed, practicing teachers and that they know all that they need to know about diverse learners. Further, they almost always continue by saying, "I have no idea why the course is required." Moreover, when surveyed, the graduate students report that they have little if any experience within cultures other than their own. Because many educators fail to understand the various backgrounds of diverse student populations, they may promote biased thinking in their classrooms based on lack of knowledge.

Curriculum in a good number of schools is slanted toward a European American point of view. In other words, institutional racism is a part of the hidden curriculum. Nieto (2004) claims that educators exclude the lives and perception of many students: "Textbooks and other materials reinforce this bias, making the development of an inclusive curriculum . . . difficult. Scrapping the existing curriculum is generally neither feasible nor practical. . . . Multicultural curriculum can be created by using the experiences, cultures, and languages of every student" (p. 408). Regardless of the subject being taught, Nieto challenges teachers to develop a variety of approaches to assure that students bring their culture to the learning environment, thus respecting and affirming all cultural differences.

## PLANNING INSTRUCTION AS PART OF THE SOLUTION

Preparing instructional units that integrate multicultural instructional methodologies reminds teachers to maintain sensitivity to as well as inclusion of all learners while planning instruction. Graduate students, all practicing teachers, were given an assignment to write an instructional unit using standards and benchmarks from their subject area curriculum. Moreover, they were required to integrate concepts from Nieto's (2004) text, *Affirming Diversity: The Sociopolitical Context of Multicultural Education*, throughout their unit plan. Students used the following framework for planning, as they created their unit: (1) write a thematic statements to guide the unit, (2) compose focus questions to support and expand the thematic statements, (3) identify specific subject area curricular content standards and benchmarks, (4) infuse multicultural concepts and strategies taken from Nieto (2004) and/or Banks (2005), and, (5) design assessment strategies and prepare instructional lesson plans. At first, some teachers struggled with the practical application of using the unit plan in the classroom. The teachers' reluctance was related to not having enough time to cover a certain amount of curriculum. However, most of the teachers agreed that the unit was part of a bigger picture and realized that the unit addressed the hidden curriculum in schools.

In addition to creating culturally responsive plans, students were encouraged to develop unit plans that would be relevant to use in their classrooms. Translating theory to practice can occur only after teachers have had the opportunity to reflect upon the theory and their teaching practices and to converse with peers about theory and practice. Integrating multicultural concepts within subject area units reinforces the premise that multicultural practices are not a stand-alone subject, but rather part of the culture and curricula for students.

## SAMPLES OF GRADUATE STUDENT UNIT PLANS

### Thematic Statement

To keep the unit congruent with the subject area and multicultural objectives selected by teachers, the graduate students wrote a thematic statement for their unit plans. An elementary school graduate teacher wrote a unit, "Exploring Our Identities," creating expectations and norms for the culture of the classroom. The thematic statement, written for the unit, included the following ideas: students will understand themselves and others as unique and important class members by sharing their heritage; students will be exposed to the importance of respecting other cultures, races, genders, religions, and ethnicities; and students will establish themselves as a community of learners (Nummer, 2005).

A high school art teacher wrote a unit called "Building Connections and Exploring Meaning through Diverse Collections of Art." The thematic statement for this unit was "Works from a diverse collection of artists to demonstrate the powerful impact that the visual arts can have in conveying what another person feels and experiences, and through that connection changes attitudes and lives" (Davis, 2004). In both these examples, teachers demonstrated the ability to use thematic statements to guide their unit planning.

### Focus Questions

Focus questions supported thematic statements and also helped teachers think about the essence of their units. A fifth grade social studies teacher wrote a unit entitled "Russian Immigrants and Their Impact." This teacher's unit focus questions included the following:

1. Where, geographically, did the immigrants come from in Russia?
2. How did they travel?
3. What struggles did they have when immigrating, and are they accepted in the area?
4. What economic forces influenced them to immigrate, and what economic contributions are they making to the area?
5. How are they shaping their new communities?
6. What are their political views? (Ward, 2005)

A high school history teacher designed a unit about the civil rights movement. The focus questions for the unit contained the following:

1. Why was the 1960s a time of great political and social reform in the United States?
2. Did desegregation in the United States win equal treatment for African-Americans?
3. What were some of the significant victories toward equality and freedom for all Americans because of the civil rights movement? (Hornbeck, 2005).

In the aforementioned examples, both of the graduate students were able to use focus questions to support their thematic statements.

*Standards and Benchmarks*

Standards and benchmarks for individual subject areas must be considered by all teachers. A middle school science teacher created an astronomy unit for sixth grade students, using state standards and benchmarks for astronomy. The teacher decided to address student intolerance for diverse cultural myths related to astronomy. Most of the students in the classroom were members of the dominant culture. The teacher noted that the students held a very biased view of the world of science based upon male western thought. Therefore, the teacher decided to blend astronomy and multicultural concepts related to tolerance. The unit objectives revolved around the study of constellations through the eyes of different cultures. The teacher included differing cultural interpretations regarding myths and names of familiar star clusters. During the culminating activity, students were expected to create and name their own constellation, while using a graph to coordinate their stars. Further, they wrote a myth about their constellation and explained its importance by stating how their own cultural beliefs influenced their stories (Hass, 2005). The intent of this teacher was to demonstrate that one group does not have a superior, subjective knowledge base over another.

### Multicultural Concepts and Strategies Taken from Nieto and/or Banks

Multicultural educational concepts and strategies, taken from Nieto (2004) and Banks (2005), were woven throughout the units. In addition to integrating multicultural concepts into unit plans, teachers became advocates for students. A high school vocational education teacher decided to conduct an analysis of a high school's "school to work" program. The teacher also identified ways in which teachers could reduce discrimination in their "school to work" program (Hyduk, 2005).

Nieto (2004) inspired this teacher to include privileges and rights for all groups of students. This teacher was alarmed when research findings indicated that 100 percent of the students participating in the work release program were White. This was disproportionate, because only 61 percent of the school's student population was White. Therefore, the teacher decided to make certain students representing all groups of students were included in the "school to work" program. To enlighten her colleagues, the teacher shared the unit plan with team members. This teacher realized that staff was guilty of institutional racism and discrimination without consciously knowing they were excluding students. Through the unit, the teacher developed lessons to ensure that employability, career development, and business management opportunities were available to all students in the school. Nieto and Banks influenced this teacher to take a deeper look at the realities in school practices and to become aware that multicultural perspectives are a very important to teachers and their students. This teacher gained knowledge of Banks's dimension regarding creating and empowering school culture so that all groups have access to opportunities.

### Lesson Plans and Assessment Strategies

Lastly, students prepared lesson plans and assessment strategies for their unit plans. A graduate teacher used literature circles as an instructional strategy to teach students about cultures, values, traditions, and experiences of others. The unit plan included three distinct lesson plans. Plans were written with the objectives to build trust, responsibility, and friendship among literature circle members. Eight more lesson plans were written to help students understand how to identify and use questioning strategies among group members. Some of the lesson plans revolved around alternative learning styles, such as thinking aloud strategies, keeping a response diary, role playing, and illustrating stories (Weaver, 2005). Thus, the teacher honored different ways students process and demonstrate what they learn. Further, the unit culminated with plans for circle members to read entire books while using literature circle strategies.

At the conclusion of the unit plans, all teachers identified a variety of assessment tools that they planned to assess their students' learning. A summary of the methods the teachers selected to use included formative and summative evaluation, teacher-made and standardized tests, projects and products, individual and collaborative work, and independent student reflections. Teachers also stated that they would use teacher observations, anecdotal notes, rubrics, student conferences, and interviews for gathering information on student achievement. An example of a high school English teacher's assessment of students' understanding of the theme of a novel could be to ask students to select portions of the text that revealed the theme to readers. Further, the teacher could gather data regarding students' comprehension of the literary element of fiction, as well as the ways in which the theme of the book exposed prejudice and bigotry. This assessment strategy would demonstrate an educator's understanding of students' different styles of communicating their learning by giving them options to answer the question. Students could self-select to write poetry, compose musical pieces, prepare reports, give speeches, and design collages to demonstrate their understanding of the learning.

## SUPPORT PROCESSES

Prior to and during preparation of their units, graduate students had ongoing opportunities to review and discuss how teachers understand student diversity and multicultural educational professional practices. Together, they explored the concepts of (1) race, (2) ethnic background, (3) family economic status, (4) gender, (5) special needs students, (6) prejudice and privilege, (7) teacher expectations regarding curriculum, instruction, and student success, and (8) the educator's individual responsibility to advocate for all groups of students. This process allowed for discourse related to the variety of issues that encompass multicultural perspectives.

## CONCLUSION

Graduate teachers identified and designed curricula, while utilizing instructional methodologies that provided sensitivity toward utilizing multicultural perspectives in their classrooms. They addressed issues at the heart of debates regarding the inclusion of a pedagogical vision that affirms the backgrounds of a diverse national population. Further, during class discussions, they stated that they understood the importance of including all points of view within the curriculum, regardless of the demographics of the student population being taught. Thus, teachers knowingly discouraged prejudice and discrimination in classrooms. Teachers realized that their responsibility is to promote opportunities for students grounded in ethical and inclusive practices. They agreed that appreciating the contributions of our nation's diverse populations and assuring equity create impartial and thoughtful learning communities. Moreover, teachers realized that their sphere of influence has sociopolitical ramifications and that they must be willing to assume responsibility as advocates for all children. Further, these graduate teachers identified professional behaviors that foster a commitment to prepare for a global society. Did the graduate students learn why the course was required? Their responses indicated that they now know about the cultural gap and how to begin to close it with their students.

## REFERENCES

Banks, J. A. (2005). *Cultural diversity and education: Foundations, curriculum, and teaching.* Boston: Allyn and Bacon.

Davis, J. (2004). Exploring diverse collections of art. Unpublished raw data.

Green, A. (1992). *Seek my face, speak my name.* Northvale, NJ: Jason Aronson.

Hass, L. (2005). Diverse cultural interpretations in astronomy. Unpublished raw data.

Hornbeck, R. (2005). Civil Rights Movement unit. Unpublished raw data.

Hyduk, N. (2005). School to work program. Unpublished raw data.

Nieto, S. (2004). *Affirming diversity: The sociopolitical context of multicultural education* (4th ed.). Boston: Pearson Education.

Nummer, S. (2005). A unit for the first weeks of school. Unpublished raw data.

Parkay, F. W., and Stanford, B. H. (2004). *Becoming a teacher* (6th ed.). Boston: Allyn & Bacon.

Sleeter, C. (2001). "Preparing teachers for culturally diverse schools: Research and the overwhelming presence of whiteness." *Journal of Teacher Education, 52*(2), 94–106.

Vasquez, H. (1996). *Skin deep study guide discussing openly race in America.* Berkeley, CA: Iris Films.

Ward, B. (2005). Russian immigrants' impact on Detroit. Unpublished raw data.

Weaver, K. (2005). Literature circles unit. Unpublished raw data.

# Teaching in Diverse Classrooms: Fact, Fiction, and Aspirations

## *Adnan Salhi*

*Teaching minorities has been a problem in the United States. Educating Arab-American minority children is more complex and problematic than educating other American minority students for political, cultural, social, racial, and historical reasons. With a special focus on the experiences of Arab-Americans in general, this chapter sheds light on the status of racism in our schools and provides specific examples drawn from the experiences of the Arab-American communities and students after September 11.*

### INTRODUCTION

Teachers and teacher candidates are faced with the urgent responsibility of transforming curricula, teaching, and assessing practices to support the learning of an increasingly diverse cultural and linguistic student population, which comes to school with a range of experiences and abilities. This learning is imperative because in the year 2000 public school students who were considered to be part of a minority group were 39 percent of the total school enrollment (National Center for Educational Statistics, 2003). Parkay and Hardcastle (2004) say "it is projected that by 2005 half of U.S. youth will be white and half will be minority" (p. 241). This demographic change in student population is in stark contrast with the demographic change in teacher population of K–12 teachers. Based on census information, Brown (2004) reports that in the year 2010, K–12 teachers will consist of 95 percent White middle-class females who have little or no cross-cultural experiences.

Teaching minorities has been a problem in the United States. Educating Arab-American minority children is more complex and problematic than educating other American minority students for political, cultural, social, racial, and historical reasons. Nieto (2004) emphasizes that in a multicultural society, "Multicultural education is a transformative process that goes far beyond cultural and linguistic maintenance. In the final analysis, multicultural education needs to confront not just issues of difference but also issues of power and privilege in society. This means challenging racism and other biases as well as the inequitable structures, policies and practices of schools and, ultimately, of society itself" (p. xxvii).

Multicultural education should be addressed in ways very different from the way it is addressed in American teacher preparation institutions. American teacher education institutions that chose to deal with the pressing issues of multicultural education did it by implementing stand-alone multicultural education courses. Unfortunately, these courses failed to achieve their intended outcomes of validating cultural diversity and student needs because, according to Brown (2004), teacher candidates take these multicultural courses and still maintain the many cultural stereotypes they held prior to going through the teacher preparation program that requires these courses. This means that such courses are of little or no significance in achieving the goals they were intended to achieve.

## THE CURRENT POLITICAL CLIMATE AND ITS IMPACT ON ARAB-AMERICAN CHILDREN

If one looks around, probably one will not find two people who will disagree that the public image of Arab-Americans is negative at best. An example of how Arab-Americans are referred to in the media is a statement made on CBS's *60 Minutes* in the Wallace Segment (1994). This statement emphasized that "The Arab is a cancer in our midst—Islamic Fundamentalists are planning to commit Holy War in the United States." This type of statement, well rooted in official rhetoric and policies of the U.S. governmental behavior toward Arab Americans, has become what Samhan (1987) calls "political racism."

In a well-known case, Detroit lawyer Abdeen Jabara, the founder of the Association of Arab-American University Graduates, was forced to file a civil rights suit against the Department of Justice for illegal electronic surveillance. Throughout the trial, the Federal Bureau of Investigation (FBI) was revealed to have conducted illegal and unwarranted investigation on Jabara. That private information was given to Israeli intelligence officials (Hagopian, 1976).

The political racism and harassments against Arab-Americans have intensified in the last couple of decades. For example, immediately after the bombing of the Oklahoma Federal Building, President Clinton and the U.S. media implicated Middle Easterners for the bombing. After 9/11, Arab-Americans were specifically targeted and dehumanized in the mainstream media and among most academes. One example of this is the portrayal of Islam as the most culturally "Other." This "Otherness" of Islam is equated with being "inimical" to "Western" values (Lewis, 2002). All of this continues to be done, obscuring decades of Western political and economic violence, intervention, colonization, and displacement and uprooting of Arabs from their homelands by Western "democracies" and colonial states they created. (An excellent documentary on this topic is "Peace, Propaganda, & the Promised Land," by Media Education Foundation, 2004.)

## STEREOTYPED, DEMONIZED, AND DEHUMANIZED

This hostile political climate prepares the public to hasten to stereotype Arab-Americans and hold them responsible for whatever reaction to U.S. foreign policies taken by anyone all over the world. This hostile political climate takes its toll on Arab-Americans in general and on Arab-American school children in particular. An example of this official hostile climate was "Operation Boulder" during the Nixon administration. This "operation" involved the Federal Bureau of Investigation (FBI), the Department of Education, the Department of Immigration and Naturalization, the Department of State, and Internal Revenue Service (IRS). The operation's directives gave government agents carte blanche to investigate Arab-American links to "terrorist activities" (Hagopian, 1976).

In a statement written for the Michigan Advisory Committee to U.S. Commission on Civil Rights (2001), Senator Carl Levin stated that, "Although passenger screening is an important component of airport safety, I am concerned that passengers of Arab descent are singled out for screening far more than other passengers. I have heard countless accounts from Arab Americans and Muslim passengers that traveling by air routinely involves humiliating and intrusive searches" (p. 4).

The Michigan Advisory Committee's observations to the U.S. government emphasized that

> *The federal government's profiling system and selective use of secret evidence may be having similar adverse effect on those in Arab and Muslim communities in this country* [emphasis original]. The permissive attitude by the federal government that allows its systems and programs to target the Arab community and the Muslim community may inadvertently be sending a message to the general populace that the Arab and Muslim communities are foreign and separate from the American mainstream, and as such are less deserving of civil rights and equal treatment. (U.S. Commission on Civil Rights, 2001, p. 22)

A stark example of how Arab-American school children pay a heavy price for the political racism is what happened in a high school in Michigan where I taught. In that school the student body is comprised of more than 80 percent Arab-Americans, but less than 15 percent of the staff were Arab-American, even though highly qualified and certified Arab-American teachers live in that community but work in far away places.

After the U.S. invasion of Iraq and capturing of Saddam Hussein, the social studies department in the school where I taught emptied its showcase to post Saddam Hussein's picture that made cover page of the Time magazine; the picture that showed him with long beard and uncombed hair. With that picture, the clear message the social studies department was sending to all the Arab-American students in the school was, "This is you! This is how we see you and this is how we treat you." The picture was standing alone in the showcase for months as if there were nothing else for the students in that school to see and learn.

## DISTANCED AND ISOLATED

In addition to being subject to racial profiling and mistreatment by official government agencies, large U.S. social groups distance themselves from Arab-Americans. The creation of a social distance between Arab-Americans and other larger American groups was confirmed by Sparrow and Chretien (1993). In their study, Sparrow and Chretien gave college students a thirty-one nation-of-origin categorization and asked them to rate groups in situations such as "gaining citizenship in your country," "moving onto your street," "entering your family by marriage," etc. Lebanese were chosen as the national origin to represent the Arabic groups.

In the overall results, Persians (Iranians who are mostly Muslims, but they are not Arabs) were ranked thirty-one in all sample groups (Blacks, Whites, men, and women). Lebanese were ranked 25/31 among Blacks, 29/31 among Whites, 28/31 among women, and 30/31 among men. In response to the questions that indicated the degree of resistance to contact with different groups, the resistance to contacting Arabs and Persians stood out clearly. Students' responses indicated that Persians would be allowed to become citizens but not to become members of any other group the respondents were affiliated with (business, clubs, neighborhood, families). Lebanese ranked slightly above Persians among Blacks who said they would accept Arabs as citizens and in the workplace, but Persians would be excluded from the workplace.

Approaching social distance differently and using it as a measure of the level of difficulty of initiation into a society, Walsh (1990) found that Arab immigrants were the least likely group to be accepted to become citizens and the most likely group to face barriers to social integration.

## DIVERSITY AND MANIPULATIONS OF THE CONCEPT OF CULTURE

The concept of culture and its manipulations by hegemonic groups and societies are very interesting. When African-Americans rose and demanded recognition of their identity and real equal rights during the civil rights movement, the dominant groups used the concepts of diversity, culture differences, and accepting others for who and what they are to dilute and water down the legitimate rights of the oppressed minorities. Not only were these legitimate demands diluted, but whatever legal rights were enforced by the civil rights movement were enjoyed mainly by already privileged social strata.

Recently, when Arabs or Muslims were involved, the ideas of accepting cultural difference and diversity were being severely attacked and the measures were reversed publicly and officially. For example, the U.S. government allegedly waged the first Gulf war against Iraq in 1991 because the latter invaded Kuwait, an act that violates the charter of United Nations and made the U.S. government feel "compelled" to take military measures to "protect" that charter.

The U.S. government did not find its occupation of Afghanistan and Iraq as violations of the charter of the United Nations or international law. Providing a total of almost $105 billion dollars to the Israeli government (McArthur, 2005) that has been occupying the Palestinian West Bank and Gaza since 1967 and subjecting the Palestinians to decades of Israeli occupation did not warrant sending the U.S. army to correct a situation that has gone egregiously wrong for long and prolonged periods of time.

After driving the Iraqi army out of Kuwait, the idea of giving the Kuwaiti people the chance to choose a democratically elected government did not even cross the mind of any of those in the U.S. administration. Therefore, it was not even mentioned. Contrary to the basic principles of democracy, the U.S. government reinstated the old Kuwaiti regime that did not allow Kuwaiti women to vote and paid no heed to any kind of human rights, thus sacrificing the basic needs of the Kuwaiti people to enjoy democracy. El-Haj (2002) cites how one American scholar of the Afghan region was interviewed by National Public Radio (NPR) in the fall of 2001 and declared the region to be one "which breeds warrior cultures" (p. 309).

As such, NPR very easily labeled the Afghans when they were fighting the U.S. foreign rule of their country as savages and uncivilized, but the U.S. military who were fighting to control Afghanistan were honorable and fighting to defend the United States. El-Haj also cites a syndicated NPR host who asked her guest, a physician who had traveled to Afghanistan for humanitarian purposes during the Taliban regime, if she had been afraid entering a culture "that is so hostile to women" (p. 309). These questions and this language about culture, as El-Haj indicated, quickly wipe out the diversity, conflicting perspectives, structural inequalities, and histories of imperialism and colonialism in the name of "other" people's uniform adherence to a way of life that seems incomprehensible to "us" (p. 309).

## A LITERACY APPROACH TO DIVERSITY

As educators, we should take the present political atmosphere and its impact on the Arab-American population very seriously because the prejudices and hostile practices against one social group have negative effects on the U.S. society as a whole. Working steadily to provide meaningful education for all learners is not only a demographic imperative, it is a political commitment that all educators must make to work toward real justice and equity in a truly diverse society.

In the teacher education classes I taught, very few of my students had a view of Arab-Americans and Muslims that was different from what they saw and heard from government agencies and mainstream media. Teaching in a mainly White Caucasian (administration and student body) rural university, I felt it one of my responsibilities as a teacher educator to expose my students to critical ways of seeing and thinking of others in general and Arab-Americans in particular. In this institution, my students were neither racist nor resistant to learn. Even though most of them were misled and misinformed, they were clever and open-minded.

Because I was teaching literacy classes, I took a literacy approach to teaching diversity and cultural understanding. Following are examples of some of the things I did in my classes that seemed effective in achieving the desired outcomes as reflected in the comments the students made in their anonymous course evaluations at the end of each semester.

Being a strong believer in the power of stories in general and personal stories in particular, I made sure to tell my students my own personal stories of growing up and how I was educated in a Palestinian society. I told them stories about how my mother, who did not have a chance to attend school during the British rule of Palestine, made sure that I did well in school. I told them stories of how my mother stayed up late doing her embroideries by the light of the kerosene lamp to earn money for the survival of her two children and to make sure that my sister and I did our homework for school before we went to bed. Such personal stories made my students see me and my community as human beings who strive for freedom, democracy, and the basic human rights that were denied to them.

I opened my students' eyes to facts of life in the places where Arab-Americans lived and worked very hard to build the U.S. economy and the U.S. society. I told them, contrary to what most of them believed, that the Arab world and Arabic societies are multi-religious and multi-ethnic. Many of my students thought that the all Arabs are Muslims. They did not know that Christianity is the second largest religion in the Arab world and that one of the pillars of Islamic faith is the belief in Christianity.

I told my college students real stories from where I worked and where I lived in the United States. I told my college students, who were mainly White Caucasians, stories like the one of the social studies department in high school where I taught. I told them the story of the public park in the neighborhood where I lived.

The city where I lived made space in one of its public parks for two fields: a baseball field and a soccer field right next to each other. The baseball field had flood lights, clean bleachers, always lined borders, and a beautiful fence. The borders of the soccer field were never marked by any lines and the goals never had any nets around them. The soccer players always had to drag the garbage containers and use them as marks for corners of the field. Another difference that marked the two adjacent fields in the same park was who used each of the fields and how often they used it. While the soccer field was very crowded and used daily by Arab-Americans who lived in the neighborhood, the baseball field was used sporadically by White Caucasians who came to play in the field from far away places in the city.

I included literature written by Arab-Americans and Muslims in all the classes I taught. The introduction of this literature was done in a needed but not forced way. For example, when we discussed universal themes of love, struggle, survival, etc., I introduced selected writings written by Arab-Americans, Chinese-Americans, or other "hyphenated" American ethnic groups that addressed the same theme and I asked my students what, if anything, did those "other" literary selections teach about the authors and whom they present or represent. I made sure to ask my students why they gave each answer they provided and how they would use these and similar pieces of literature in their own teachings.

When we talked about literacy and how it is a socially constructed skill, I planned and organized my class activities to provide opportunities of learning about different social groups and cultures from the sources that are part of the concerned social groups and cultures. For example, every time I taught literature circles, I provided novels and short stories by Arab and Muslim writers to be read, discussed in the groups, and shared with the entire class. I asked my students to look for books written by Arab writers and published in English. When my students were surprised by the scant number of sources available on Arab-Americans and written by Arabs or Arab-Americans, we discussed the political, social, and educational effects this lack of sources could have on American perceptions of Arabs if the only source in this area had a hostile predisposition.

Starr (1991) pointed to the lack of sensitivity to Arabic culture in the American public schools and universities. He wrote that although "Arabic is the language of one of the world's great civilizations, and one to which the West has been profoundly indebted for over a millennium in fields as diverse as mathematics, chemistry, geography, and philosophy" (p. B2), no effort or commitment was made in the curriculum of American education to reflect the contributions of Arabs and Muslims to Western civilizations.

Because Arabic culture is "referred to in only negative ways" (Nieto, 1996, p. 137) in the American public schools, "all students are miseducated to the extent that they receive only a partial and biased education. The primary victims of biased education are those who are invisible in the curriculum" (Nieto, 1996, p. 213). Therefore, it is the responsibility of educators who sincerely believe in justice for all to educate themselves about all social groups from the primary sources that represent these groups.

In their anonymous course evaluations, students very often made reference to the diversity issues they learned in my literacy classes. One student wrote "I really enjoyed your classes. I felt they were informative and non-threatening. They also gave me a sense of being culturally diverse in a class that did not reflect this trait in the population. We need to be culturally sensitive to allow our students to succeed." Another student wrote "I really enjoyed coming to class every week which is a big compliment since the class is on Saturday morning. I found Dr. Salhi's teaching methods extremely useful. I plan on using his methods in my own class one day. I also enjoyed hearing Dr. Salhi talk about Palestine and his journey to America. I feel like I became more cultured in his class."

## REFERENCES

Brown, E. L. (2004). "What precipitates change in cultural awareness during a multicultural course: The message or the method?" *Journal of Teacher Education, 55*(4), 325–40.

El-Haj, T. R. A. (2002). "Contesting the politics of culture." *Anthropology & Education Quarterly, 33*(3), 308–16.

Hagopian, H. (1976). "Minority rights in a nation state: The Nixon administration's campaign against Arab-Americans." *Journal of Palestine Studies, 5*(1–2), 97–115.

Lewis, B. (2002). *What went wrong? Western impact and Middle Eastern response.* Oxford: Oxford University Press.

Media Education Foundation. (2004). *Peace, propaganda & the promised land.* Available online from www.mediaed.org.

McArthur, S. (April 2005). "Total direct aid to Israel conservatively estimated at almost $105 billion." *The Washington Report on Middle East Affairs, April, 24*(3), 16–17.

National Center for Educational Statistics. (2003). *The Condition of Education.* Retrieved March 14, 2003, from http://nces.ed.gov/programs/coe/.

Nieto, S. (1996). *Affirming diversity: The sociological context of multicultural education* (2nd ed.). New York: Longman.

Nieto, S. (2004). *Affirming diversity: The sociological context of multicultural education* (4th ed.). Boston: Pearson Education.

Parkay, F. W., and Hardcastle, S. B. (2004). *Becoming a teacher* (6th ed.). Boston: Allyn & Bacon.

Samhan, H. H. (1987). "Politics and exclusion: The Arab-American experience." *Journal of Palestine Studies, 26*(2), 11–28.

Sparrow, K. H., and Chretien, D. M. (1993). "The social distance perceptions of racial and ethnic groups by college students." *Sociological Spectrum, 13,* 277–88.

Starr, S. F. (April 10, 1990). "Colleges can help America overcome its ignorance of Arab language and culture [Opinion]." *The Chronicle of Higher Education,* B2.

U.S. Commission on Civil Rights, Midwestern Regional Office. (2001). *Civil rights issues facing Arab Americans in Michigan.* ED 457-277.

Walsh, A. (1990). "Becoming American and liking it as a function of social distance." *Sociological Inquiry, 60*(2), 177–89.

Wallace, M. (November 12, 1994). "The Notebook," *60 Minutes.*

# About the Contributors

**Adnan Salhi, Ed.D.**, earned his doctorate from Wayne State University in Michigan. He taught English, math, science, and foreign languages in several countries in elementary, middle and high schools. He has many national and international publications and refereed presentations and takes on leading roles in several professional organizations. His research interests include effective teaching and learning, literacy, motivation to read and write, and the effective use of technology in teaching and learning. After serving as an associate professor at Marygrove College and Saginaw Valley State University, he currently teaches reading and Arabic as a foreign language at Henry Ford Community College. Dr. Salhi received research awards and he is presently conducting research applying single subject experimental design to reading and teacher education. He welcomes collaboration and can be reached at: asalhi26271@hfcc.edu, or adnan_salhi@yahoo.com.

**P. Rudy Mattai, Ph.D.**, is professor of educational foundations, SUNY-College at Buffalo, Buffalo, New York and is currently president (2006–2009) of the Global Federation of the Associations for Teacher Education (GloFATE) and immediate past president (2006–2007) of the Association for Teacher Educators (USA). He is the editor of *Child Studies* Journal. His research areas are race and ethnic issues in education and urban education and has published widely in both areas. He has received numerous awards and consults nationally and internationally on diversity issues and program development and evaluation. Contact: prmattai@att.net.

**Jacqueline M. Williams, Ed.S.**, is currently completing an Ed.D. in curriculum and instruction with an emphasis on the gifted and talented. She has been an instructor in exceptional education in public schools in New York and

Florida and has taught in both traditional and non traditional classrooms. She is actively engaged in school board administration and pursues research activities in the area of the gifted and talented. She has received numerous academic awards including the Certificate of Excellence Award and a Minority Fellowship Award, SUNY-College at Buffalo, Buffalo, New York. Contact: j.arms@daystar.net.

**Han Liu, Ph.D.**, is currently an assistant professor in the Department of Education at Marygrove College, Detroit, Michigan. Dr. Han Liu worked as teacher, curriculum developer, methodology researcher, and education administrator in various K–12 educations settings. Educational technology is one of his major research areas with a focus on online learning. He can be reached at lliuhan@gmail.com.

**Karen Schulte, Sp.A.**, is an assistant professor in the Department of Special Education at Eastern Michigan University in Ypsilanti, Michigan. Her primary area of expertise is learning disabilities. She worked for twenty-seven years in the K–12 public school system, both as a teacher and as a coordinator of professional development, prior to joining the faculty at Eastern Michigan University.

**Sandy Alber, Ed.D.**, associate professor, teaches theory, development, ecology, culture, family, advocacy and action research courses to students seeking Doctoral and Masters Degrees at Oakland University, where she has been nominated for excellence in teaching and research awards. Her scholarly interests are similar to her teaching interests. She writes and speaks about parenting, social justice, advocacy, action research, teacher development, and early mathematics. Her commitment to the Association of Teacher Educators is strong. She currently serves on several state and national committees, on the Council of Unit Presidents and on the Executive Board. She is the current President of the Michigan Association of Teacher Educators.

**Sally Edgerton-Netke, Ed.D.**, was professor at Saginaw Valley State University, specialized in early childhood education. She was a frequent presenter and contributor in this area as well as an active member of the NAEYC locally, state-wide, and nationally. As past President of the Michigan Early Childhood Education Consortium, she leaves a strong legacy. Sally lost her battle with cancer August, 2005.

**Bess Kypros, Ed.D.**, is a professor of education at Madonna University, a private Catholic University in Livonia, Michigan. She is the coordinator of the

Child Development, Early Childhood Education and Family and Consumer Science programs. For the past fifteen years Dr. Kypros has been engaged in collaborative research with two other colleagues from state universities regarding action research. She is a regular presenter at early childhood and education conferences and a contributor to educational journals.

**Pamela Morehead, Ph.D.**, is a faculty member in the Teacher Education Department at Oakland University in Rochester, MI. She is a former elementary principal and teacher consultant. Her research interests include teacher leadership and professional development. Her earned degrees are in special education, early childhood, and educational leadership. Dr. Morehead presents at local, state and national conferences. Her current studies include examining the conceptions prospective teachers have about quality teaching and digital storytelling for prospective teachers.

**Jumanne Sledge, Ed.D.**, is the president of World Class Leadership Academy, LLC., an educational consultant firm and visiting professor of education at Oakland University. He is a former teacher, principal, and central office administrator. His interests are in the areas of school reform and improvement and urban education. His commitments toward closing the achievement gap and social justice have created opportunities for him to present several local, national, and international conferences while consulting with school districts throughout the nation.

**Anne Tapp, Ph.D.**, an associate professor at Saginaw Valley State University in Michigan, specializes in curriculum and instruction, technology and science education at the early childhood and elementary levels. She is a frequent presenter and contributor within these areas. Anne has served as a NASA Solar System Educator since 1999 which includes her initial selection as one of ten STARDUST Fellows.

**Poonam Kumar, Ph.D.**, is an associate professor in the department of Educational Technology and Development at Saginaw Valley State University in Michigan. She teaches educational technology and special education courses. She has presented at national and international conferences and has authored several articles related to technology integration in teacher education.

**Elizabeth A. Hansen, Ph.D.**, is a professor of education and is the chair of the Educational Technology and Development Department within Saginaw Valley State University's College of Education. Her areas of expertise include technology, educational leadership, and e-learning. She serves on the board for the Consortium for Outstanding Achievement in Teaching with Technology (COATT).

**Guidi Yang, Ph.D.**, earned her doctorate in Reading Education from the State University of New York at Buffalo. She has taught teacher education courses in reading at Lake Superior State University. Her main research interests are reading processes, reading strategies, and instructional approaches to reading development for both native and non-native English speakers. She is also interested in preservice teachers' knowledge development in reading instruction.

**Naomi Jeffery Petersen, Ed.D**, Central Washington University, chairs and teaches in the Secondary Education and Foundations. She continues to develop the Mathematical Teaching Profile. Other scholarly projects focus on the use of cognitive tools for learning and classroom assessment, and the scholarship of teaching and learning in higher education. She serves as an external evaluator for grants. She welcomes collaboration and can be reached at NJP@cwu.edu.

**Finney Cherian, Ph.D.**, is currently an assistant professor of language arts with the faculty of education at the University of Windsor (Canada). He has been a classroom teacher and teacher educator within Canada and the United States. Dr. Cherian's research explores the complexities of teaching social justice and critical literacy within schools and teacher education programs. He is a graduate of the Ontario Institute for Studies in Education/University of Toronto.

**Karen Bolak, Ed.D.**, is an assistant professor at Oakland University. She specializes in multicultural education, teacher preparation, educational studies and leadership. Dr. Bolak's contributions in the school setting include: teaching, serving as a central office professional development consultant, and administration. She serves the community as an advocate for children, families, and educators. Dr. Bolak writes and speaks about relationships that affect schooling, curriculum development, leadership, and adult support of youth.